hopscotch

Playing the game

Player 1 tosses his/her marker into
Square 1, being careful to land
exactly in the square and not on the
lines or outside otherwise you forfeit
your turn. Then Player 1 hops through
the course skipping the square with
the marker in it on the way to home
base (single squares are for hopping
and the double squares (4, 5 and 7, 8)
can have both feet planted). At home
base you turn around and do the course
in reverse, collecting your marker
on the way back. If you successfully
complete the course, you continue onto
Square 2 and 3 etc.

If you step on a line, miss a square,
lose your balance or don't land your
marker within the appropriate square
during your go, you forfeit your turn
and, when it is your go again, you
start where you left off.

The other players, in turn, go through
the same process until one player (the
winner) has successfully completed
the course (placing their marker in
every square and hopping through each
sequence, forward and reverse).

Photography by Greg Elms

Lisa McCune

with Di Thomas

Hopscotch and Honey Joys

FOOD FOR YOUR FAMILY AND FRIENDS

ALLEN&UNWIN

Allen & Unwin
83 Alexander Street
Crows Nest NSW 2065
Australia
Phone: (61 2) 8425 0100
Fax: (61 2) 9906 2218
Email: info@allenandunwin.com
Web: www.allenandunwin.com

Cataloguing-in-Publication details are available
from the National Library of Australia
www.trove.nla.gov

ISBN: 978 1 74237 415 4 (pbk.)

Project management by Tracy O'Shaughnessy
Design by 21-19 (www.21-19.com)
Photography by Greg Elms
Styling by Fiona Hammond
Printed in China at Everbest Printing Co.
10 9 8 7 6 5 4 3 2 1

To Dame, Jaye, Asher and
Jem. Here's a little time
capsule to treasure forever ...
Thanks for helping to create it.
- Di

Archer, Oliver and Remy, thank
you for choosing me as your
mum. I quite simply adore you.
To my partner in crime, Tim ...
you are the cornflour that thickens
my sauce.
- Lisa

Contents

mum

lisa about di

Di and her husband Damian are both childhood friends of my husband Tim. I first met Di as she and Damian were heading off around Australia and the world. That was in 1997. It was on their return that I got to know Di. Since then, I guess our lives have grown and changed at the same pace. We bought and renovated our first homes around the corner from each other in 1998/1999, got married in 2000/2001, then started having babies from 2001 to 2006. Di understands what family is all about; it's inherent in her upbringing. Her home is always filled with voices and laughter, friends and food. And she manages it with ease. So here we are, in 2010, having talked each other through the often-trying moments of six children under the age of five. The sleep deprivation has improved (I still have a coffee addiction) and I am looking forward to the next chapter with eyes wide open. Cheers, Di!

di about Lisa

Damian and I met Lisa when she got together with our good friend Tim. We all lived close by and spent our spare time helping each other renovate and decorate our houses, and hosting long lunches that would often evolve into longer dinners. At the time Lisa was fast becoming famous, but to us she was just our quirky mate, who loved a laugh and a challenge and was always trialling a new dessert on us, which my husband would always take great pleasure in scoring out of ten—very harshly, I might add! I love that Lisa is a far more experimental cook than me. I guess I'm more traditional in that I continually fall back on what I know and grew up with. As always, Lisa makes any task, no matter how big or small, fun and achievable. She's by far and away the most motivated person I know, and whilst making this book she managed to juggle starring in a stage show, developing a screen-play, various TV, magazine and radio commitments … the list goes on! I can't thank her enough for asking me to be a part of this project and for her wonderful and forever supportive friendship.

Introduction

Putting this book together has certainly been an interesting exercise in actually trying to write down all our usual guesstimations; pinches, hand-fuls, touches of and sploshes had to somehow transform into cups and tablespoons!

Upfront we agreed that we weren't going to try and reinvent the wheel. We're not professional cooks or Master Chefs, and we don't want to try to pass ourselves off as such. We're just two friends, who are both mums and who love food and home cooking. Since becoming parents, we reckon that together with our partners we've been responsible for preparing well over 26,000 meals. It's a tricky business, catering for a child's taste buds. One day they like avocado, the next it's discarded with disdain... But from years of reading, experimenting with and collecting recipes, as well as relying on those memories of helping out our own mums in the kitchen, here are some of our favourite tried and tested recipes.

Our kids, now four, five, six, seven, eight and nine years old, have pro-gressed beyond baby food, and while they're still young and therefore essentially 'fussy' eaters, it's a marvellous time for us to incorporate a wider range of flavours and variety into our everyday meals. We aim to please most of the people most of the time, which is all you can ever ask for really!

Many of our recipes are flexible, so feel free to play around with them or drop the odd ingredient if it's not your favourite thing. Most importantly, grab a pen or pencil and scribble your own notes on these pages—a slightly different cooking time to suit your own oven, an alternative serving sugges-tion, a recipe from a friend—go ahead and add to it because as mums and dads, we never stop learning and sharing.

Hope you enjoy!
Lisa and Di

Kitchen tools

I have journeyed into the depths of my kitchen cupboards and drawers to compile a list of my most favoured and used kitchen items. — Lisa

KNIVES
Good, sharp knives are essential. You develop your favourites. Mine are: a paring knife, a large cutting knife, a bread knife and a serrated tomato knife.

WOODEN BOARDS
A friend, who is a chef, was horrified to see me using my knives on a glass cutting board. He bought a wooden board for me, which I still use. I now use the glass one for meat preparation and the wooden board for everything else. Oil your wooden board every now and then for a treat. This is one of the most used items in the house.

PEELERS
Throw out the old one and buy a new one if it's not sharp. Also, a soft fruit peeler is handy for summer fruits and tomatoes.

ZESTER
This small utensil is used for removing the peel from citrus fruits; it's safer than a grater and preserves fingers and skin!

CORER
Great for apples and tomatoes, this simple tool will quickly remove the centre of the fruit, saving you having to cut around it.

KITCHEN SCISSORS
These are used every day in my kitchen — for cutting up a pizza or herbs, or a chicken, or marshmallow ...

COOKING SPOONS
Having a variety of wooden spoons, spatulas and serving spoons is essential. My kitchen drawer is a tangled web of items, which are all used ... it's my girl shed. My favourite is a wooden rice paddle from Cobargo in New South Wales.

MEASURES
A set of cup measures, some spoon measures, a pyrex jug for liquids and kitchen scales is my basic set-up.

Baking dishes, pots and pans
I end up using the same dishes and pans over and over, even though I look adoringly in the Minimax window every time I walk past. I regularly use my muffin tray, my heavy-based saucepan (an investment piece), a couple of good stainless steel pots in different sizes and my springform cake tin. A set of ramekins are also extremely good to have on hand for preparing, baking and serving.

ALUMINIUM SPRAY BOTTLES
I have two. One is for olive oil and the other is for balsamic vinegar. When you are cooking or making salads, spray bottles distribute a finer, more even spread. I bought mine at the local $2 shop.

ELECTRIC MIXER
A good mixer leaves your hands free to get on with other things. It also physically does what only a superwoman could do with a stirring arm. I haven't used the bread hook attachment, but I will one day.

RICE COOKER
I'm very, very happy with the rice cooker. The fact that it keeps the rice warm after it's cooked is brilliant when there's a crowd over for dinner.

CANDY (SUGAR) THERMOMETER
I discovered this handy little tool while putting this book together. It really is great for the sweet stuff.

YOGHURT MAKER
I will use it this year, Mum! (Christmas present 2007)

'Feeling peckish? Me too. I'd walk
a mile for one of those yummy
little'...

Smoothies

3 cups milk
¾ cup yoghurt, natural or other and/or
¾ cup ice-cream
2 bananas and/or washed berries (strawberries and blueberries are nice)
2 tbsp honey or maple syrup or
½ cup Milo for a chocolate version

Smoothies are great for breakfast, lunch or afternoon tea. What's more, they're packed with goodness and yummy to slurp on. Barely a day goes by in our house without some form of smoothie being whipped up. In summer, mangoes and fresh berries top the list; in winter, we belt through the bananas. The combinations are endless and it's a terrific way to use up some of that fruit that's looking a little lonely—with a splash of honey or maple syrup, even some peanut butter for those without nut issues.

I prefer to use yoghurt in my morning smoothies, and a little ice-cream in the afternoon to thicken them up. We have put together a basic flavour suggestion here, but experiment a little. If the number of kids passing through increases, double the quantities.
— *Lisa*

1. Blend all the ingredients in a blender until smooth.
2. Pour into glasses and serve with a straw.

Serves 4

A2 MILK
You may have seen A2 milk at
the supermarket. Naturally rich
in the A2 type of beta casein
protein, which is the original
milk protein, there has been
a lot of discussion about its
health benefits. Do some reading
on it; I'm certainly a convert.
- Lisa

Lemonade

¾ cup sugar
1 cup water
1 cup lemon juice (strain the juice
  if the kids don't like bits)
4 cups soda water or water
  mint

A few years ago, some family friends moved into a house with twelve lemon trees bordering their fence-line. The kids had such a great time collecting the bountiful supply of lemons, then making lemonade. Those trees provided hours of entertainment and sticky fun.

— Lisa

1. Heat the sugar and water in a saucepan until the sugar dissolves.
2. Add the lemon juice to the dissolved mixture and stir through.
3. Mix the lemon syrup with water or soda water and refrigerate until chilled.
4. To serve, add a hint of mint garnish for those who like it and, if weather permits, toss in some ice cubes.

Serves 4

SUMMER FUN
My kids have had some
great fun in summer
making ice cubes with
mint or tiny flowers
frozen inside. You could
also try the curly zest
of some oranges or lemons.
- Lisa

LEMON ON ICE
If you have an over-supply of
lemons, squeeze the juice and
freeze it in ice cube trays.
Once frozen, transfer the cubes
to freezer bags. They're great for
cooking with, and for drinks in
summer. The lemon rind will also
keep if you can be bothered to
grate and freeze it.

Frozen Fruit Cups

⅓ cup sugar
½ cup water
2 cups strawberries or other fruit,
    pureed in a blender
1 cup apple or orange juice (use
    fresh or bought), or lemonade
    icy pole moulds, or paper cups
    with popsicle sticks

On a 40 degree day, in the late afternoon, when there's not a breath of wind (and you can't run under the sprinkler to cool down), reach for a frozen fruit cup. They might be watermelon, strawberry, apple, berry, orange …
— *Lisa*

1. Combine the sugar and water in a saucepan and heat to make a syrup.
2. Once the sugar is dissolved, combine the syrup with the pureed fruit and juice or lemonade.
3. Pour the mixture into the moulds or cups. If using a plastic/paper cup, cut out a cardboard disc (to act as a lid) with a slit for a popsicle stick to be inserted. Put the moulds or cups in the freezer to set. This should take approximately 6–8 hours.

Serves 8

FRUIT
It is fitting to include fruit
in our section on Snacks. In
our household it is the one
food that has to be constantly
restocked. If it's on the
bench at eye height, it just
disappears.
-Lisa

Chocolate Chip Cookies

250 g butter, chopped and softened
⅔ cup firmly packed brown sugar
½ cup caster sugar
2 eggs
1 tsp vanilla essence
2½ cups plain flour
1 tsp bicarbonate of soda
1½ cups chocolate bits

Don't you just love the aroma of baking biscuits? That's usually my inspiration to get baking. These cookies are quick, easy and delicious, but above all I find that I've always got these ingredients in my pantry.
— *Di*

1. Preheat the oven to 190°C.
2. Beat the butter, sugars, eggs and vanilla essence with an electric mixer.
3. Add the flour, bicarbonate of soda and chocolate. Stir to combine.
4. Put heaped teaspoons of the mixture onto lined oven trays, allowing room for the biscuits to spread.
5. Bake in the preheated oven for 8–10 minutes, or until lightly browned.
6. Cool the cookies on their trays for a few minutes before transferring them to a wire rack.

Makes about 60 cookies

Chewy Anzac Biscuits

1 cup plain flour
1 cup rolled oats
1 cup desiccated coconut
¾ cup (firmly packed) brown sugar
125 g butter
3 tbsp golden syrup
2 tbsp water
1 tsp bicarbonate of soda

In 2010, I attended my first Anzac Day Dawn Service with my eldest son. In the cold darkness of that April morning we stood and we listened and I thought of those mothers who sent their sons off to war—and I cried. Lest we forget.

This is Di's chewy Anzac biscuits recipe. They are yummy!

— Lisa

1. Preheat the oven to 160°C.
2. Sift the flour into a large bowl. Stir in the oats, coconut and brown sugar.
3. Put the butter, golden syrup and water in a saucepan and stir over a low heat until melted. Stir in the bicarbonate of soda.
4. Pour the butter mixture into the bowl of dry ingredients and mix until everything is combined.
5. Place tablespoons of the mixture onto lined baking trays (approximately 5 cm apart). Flatten each biscuit with the back of a fork.
6. Bake in the preheated oven for 5 minutes. Pull out the trays and give the biscuits another flatten with the fork. Return the trays to the oven for a further 3–5 minutes.
7. Cool the Anzacs firstly on their trays, then transfer to a wire rack.

Makes about 30 biscuits

WHAT'S IN A NAME?
So why are these biscuits called Anzacs? During WWI, women would send biscuits to their men overseas. They were concerned about their nutrition, and as these biscuits have an oat base and no eggs, they wouldn't spoil and were ideal to transport in airtight tins. After the landing at Gallipoli, these 'Soldiers Biscuits' became Known as 'Anzacs'.

French Toast

4 tbsp milk
5 eggs
1 block loaf of bread cut into
   ½ inch slices
1 tbsp butter
icing sugar/maple syrup and
   berries to serve

My partner makes this yummy French Toast. I really like eating it. He prepares it the night before, so it's ready first thing—it's great for special occasions.
— *Lisa*

1. Combine the milk and eggs and beat with a fork.
2. Soak the bread pieces in the egg and milk mix, cover and leave in the fridge overnight.
3. Place the butter in a non-stick frying pan over a medium heat.
4. Add the bread to the pan and cook on both sides until golden brown.
5. Dust the toast with icing sugar and serve with a drizzle of maple syrup and berries on the side.

Serves 5

Fear less, hope more;
Eat less, chew more;
Whine less, breathe more;
Talk less, say more;
Love more, and all good
things will be yours.
—Swedish proverb

CODDLED EGGS

We were given a set of coddlers for our wedding. They are small porcelain cups with a lid. A raw egg is cracked inside each buttered cup, then you add whatever you like ... salt and pepper, cheese, chives, ham. After putting on the lid, you place the coddler in a saucepan of boiling water for 7-8 minutes and the coddled eggs are ready to eat, straight from the coddler. They're such a tasty variation on the brekkie egg and easy to prepare the night before.
- Lisa

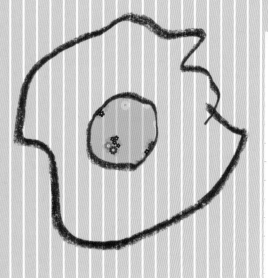

BREKKIE WRAPS

Brekkie wraps are a good weekend solution for a busy crowd. Grab some soft tortilla wraps, splash in a little chutney and throw in some cooked egg and bacon, some avocado, a sprinkle of cheese and a hint of mesculun. You can toast it in a sandwich press for a few minutes, then wrap it up and take it away. These wraps are a great start to a road trip or a morning at the footy.

Vegie Sticks & Hummus

hummus
400 g can chickpeas, drained but
  with liquid set aside
1 clove garlic, crushed
2 tbsp olive oil
2 tbsp lemon juice
sprinkle of cumin
sprinkle of sea salt
1 tbsp tahini (optional—my kids
  find the taste a little strong)
  parsley

1 carrot, cut into sticks
1 capsicum, sliced
1 handful snowpeas
1 stick celery, thinly sliced
  flatbread, sliced

My kids are always scratching around for snacks just before dinner. So when the 'Have a glass of water' line doesn't satisfy, and the groans become deeper and more terrifying, chopped up vegies and a dollop of hummus in a bowl does the trick. The hummus keeps for about five days in the fridge and packs nicely into a school lunch box with a slice of flatbread.
— Lisa

1. To make the hummus, place the drained chickpeas in a blender or food processor and puree, adding the garlic, olive oil, lemon juice, cumin, salt and tahini if you're using it. If you like a smoother hummus, add some of the reserved liquid from the chickpeas.
2. Garnish with parsley for the grown-ups and serve with the vegie sticks and flatbread.

Stuffed Potatoes

6 potatoes, medium-sized
175 g can corn kernels
3 middle bacon rashers, chopped
⅔ cup grated cheddar cheese
2 tbsp sour cream
1 tbsp chopped chives
salt and pepper
6 thin slices cheddar cheese

Spuds. How can you go wrong? You could pretty much put anything into these sure-fire little packages. Great as a snack, side dish or a main meal, even fussy little eaters will love these.
— Di

1. Wrap the potatoes in foil and bake in a preheated oven at 200°C for about an hour.
2. Combine all the remaining ingredients (except for the sliced cheese) in a bowl.
3. Unwrap the baked potatoes and slice off the tops.
4. Scoop out most of the flesh, adding two-thirds of this to the filling mixture.
5. Spoon the filling back into the skins, piling it up in a mound.
6. Top the stuffed potatoes with a thin slice of cheese before returning to the oven for a further 10–15 minutes.

Makes 6 stuffed potatoes

KING EDWARD
Long and oval in shape, this common potato is great for roasting and baking, and because of its creamy flesh it makes fluffy baked potatoes. Choose another variety for salads.

SEBAGO
Sebago is a good all-purpose potato. Long, white and oval in appearance, it is excellent for boiling and mashing.

PONTIAC
Pontiac is a round, red-skinned potato with white flesh. It is excellent for mashing and also good in cold salads as it holds its shape after cooking. It is not really suitable for frying.

COLIBAN
A common potato, with a floury textured flesh, the coliban is good for baking, roasting and mashing.

DESIREE
The desiree is a round and pink potato with pale yellow waxy flesh. It is good for boiling, mashing and roasting and terrific for salads.

potatoes

There are many varieties of the spud. Easy and delicious, they feed a nation. — Lisa

NICOLA
This long, oblong-shaped potato with yellowish skin and firm flesh is a good all-purpose potato.

DUTCH CREAM
Dutch cream potatoes are very common in Australia. Large and oval in shape, they have a yellow, waxy flesh and are really good for mashing and roasting.

KIPFLER
A long potato with a buttery flavour and waxy flesh, the kipfler is terrific in salads, or for baking and boiling. It is not a good mashing or frying potato.

ROYAL BLUE
The royal blue has a purple appearance, with white flesh. It is a good general-purpose potato.

Nachos

1 packet corn chips
tomato salsa, bought or homemade
  (see recipe below)
cheddar cheese, grated
avocado
sour cream

tomato salsa
1 tbsp olive oil
½ red onion, finely chopped
4 tomatoes, deseeded and skins
  removed
1 tbsp lemon juice
2 tsp brown sugar
salt and pepper to taste

After school or at the weekend, nachos are always a hit. The kids can pretty much put this together themselves—just help them out with the oven component. Individual bowls can be a useful way to prepare and serve nachos when catering for differing tastebuds. Heaven help the mother who puts on too much avocado and not enough cheese.

— *Lisa*

1. Preheat the oven to 180°C.
2. Place the corn chips in individual ovenproof bowls. Pour over the salsa and sprinkle with the grated cheese.
3. Bake in the oven for approximately 10 minutes, or until the chips are warm and the cheese is melted.
4. Mash the avocado with a fork and add a pinch of salt or pepper if desired.
5. Remove the bowls from the oven and dollop with avocado and sour cream.
6. Eat while warm.

tomato salsa
1. In a saucepan, sauté the red onion in the olive oil until soft.
2. Add the tomatoes, lemon juice, brown sugar and salt and pepper to taste.
3. Puree the mix in a blender or food processor.

Serves 6 small ramekin bowls

SKINNING AND DESEEDING TOMATOES

To skin tomatoes, place them in a saucepan of boiling water. When the skins start to split, remove the tomatoes from the pan and immerse in a tub of cold water. When cool to the touch, remove the tomatoes from the cold water and peel off the skin. To remove the seeds, simply halve the tomato and spoon out the seeds. You can also use a knife to peel around the seed core.

Calamari

500 g calamari in 5 ml thick rings,
   tenderised
1 cup cornflour
1 tsp paprika
salt and pepper
vegetable oil for shallow frying

dipping sauce

for the kids

2 tbsp mayonnaise
1 tsp Dijon mustard
1 tbsp lemon juice
1 tbsp white wine vinegar

for us

2 tbsp mayonnaise
1 tsp minced chilli
1 tbsp white wine vinegar
1 tbsp chopped chives

I can imagine eating this while sitting at a little wooden table and chairs alongside a pebbled shore on a quiet Greek island in the Ionian…

This calamari is a quick and easy side dish or starter that's loved by both adults and kids. Its success is completely dependant on the quality of your seafood, so find a friendly fishmonger who you can trust and who is happy to perhaps slice the rings to order.
— Di

1. Dust the calamari rings in the combined dry ingredients.
2. Shallow fry the calamari in batches in a pan of heated oil until golden brown all over.
3. Serve on a bed of rocket leaves with lemon wedges, sea salt and perhaps a dipping sauce …

Serves 3 as an entree

QUALITY AND QUANTITY

When shopping for seafood, there are
a couple of things to keep in mind.
A good guide for quantity is 250 g
per adult serve, adjusted accordingly
for kids. Popular fish for families
include flathead fillets or tails,
flake, hapuka and rockling. Calamari
and prawns are also well-loved.
Your fishmonger will be your
best source of information and
inspiration on cooking tips and
how to keep seafood fresh for as
long as possible once you get
it home.

Ham, Cheese & Asparagus Mini Croissants

½ cup ham off the bone, shredded
½ cup grated cheddar cheese
5 asparagus spears, blanched and
   finely chopped
salt and pepper
2 sheets ready-rolled puff pastry
1 egg, lightly beaten

Give these cute and tasty croissants a go and experiment with your favourite fillings. They are delicious at any time of day.
— Di

1. Preheat the oven to 180°C.
2. Combine the ham, cheese, asparagus and seasoning in a bowl.
3. Cut each pastry sheet into quarters, then slice each quarter diagonally to make 8 triangles per sheet.
4. Place a dessertspoon of filling across the base of each triangle. Roll up from the base and shape into a small crescent.
5. Place the croissants onto a lined baking tray and brush with egg.
6. Bake in the preheated oven for 12–15 minutes.

Makes 16 croissants

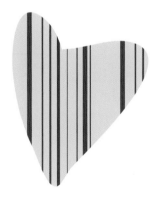

Tuna Sausage Rolls with Wasabi Mayo

filling
4 eggs, lightly beaten
1 large onion, grated
1 cup thickened cream
2 cloves garlic, crushed
1 cup chopped parsley (roughly
  1 bunch)
2 cups grated cheddar cheese
1 packet plain water crackers,
  crushed (in a bag with a rolling
  pin is best—a rough consistencyis
  what's required, so don't crush
  them all to dust!)
1 cup canned tuna in brine, drained

3 ready-rolled puff pastry sheets,
  cut in half
1 extra egg, lightly beaten
sesame seeds

wasabi mayo dipping sauce
1 cup whole egg mayonnaise
1 large lemon, juiced
½ tube (or more if desired)
wasabi paste
cracked pepper

Having never eaten canned tuna in my life, I was completely blown away when I first tried these deliciously more-ish sausage rolls. It's the wasabi mayo that's the real winner for me, and I recommend individual bowls for multiple dipping!
— Di

1. Preheat the oven to 200°C.
2. Mix all the filling ingredients together in a bowl.
3. Divide the mixture into six equal portions.
4. Place the mixture along each pastry sheet and roll to enclose, with a little of the extra egg helping to seal the seam. Keep the seam on the underside of the rolls.
5. Brush each roll with the lightly beaten egg and sprinkle with sesame seeds.
6. Cut each roll into 5 or 6 pieces and arrange on a lined baking tray.
7. Bake in the preheated oven for about 30 minutes, or until golden brown.
8. Combine the ingredients for wasabi mayo and serve with the tuna rolls.

Makes 30–36 rolls

herbs

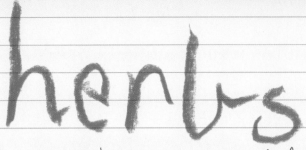

Here are some of the more popular herbs that can be used in cooking, planted in your garden or potted and given as living gifts. — Lisa

ROSEMARY
Rosemary has a strong flavour, so only small amounts are needed in cooking. It is a good herb to use for meat marinades, or simply tie a sprig to a roast lamb. It is best to cook fresh rosemary to soften the spiky leaves, or use dried. Rosemary grows well in pots or garden beds.

BASIL
Basil has a sweet influence in food and is used widely. It is particularly well-suited to Italian pasta sauces as it goes so well with tomatoes. It is also used for making pesto. Basil can be grown in garden beds or in pots and will grow indoors.

CHIVES
Chives are from the onion group of plants. Add them to soups, salads or egg dishes for a light onion flavour. They also make a great garnish. Chives grow well in pots.

MINT
You may have mint growing wild in your garden. It has a fresh flavour and can be added to salads, drinks or sauces. It can be grown in pots and is easier to contain that way.

PARSLEY
Parsley is a great herb to add to savoury dishes or to sprinkle over food before serving. It also makes a pretty, edible garnish. The continental

(flat leaf) variety has a different look and taste to its crinkled cousin, but both will grow in a garden bed or a pot.

THYME
Said to be the herb of motherhood, thyme has a very distinctive taste and aroma. A sprig added to meat dishes will infuse beautifully. There is a lemon-scented thyme available.

OREGANO
Oregano has a similar appearance to marjoram, but a more bitter taste. Chop it finely for use in food. Again, oregano is a good herb for use in Italian food.

BAY LEAVES
Bay leaves come from the bay tree, which can grow to 12 metres, so a potted gift would be on the larger side. The leaves (you only need one or two) impart a beautiful flavour in slow-cooked meals.

DILL
Dill has a really distinctive smell and taste and is great with seafood. It's a beautiful, fluffy-looking plant but harder to keep in a pot. I buy this one when I need it.

CORIANDER
Coriander is used a lot in Indian, Middle Eastern and Asian foods. It has a sweet aroma and taste and is great with fish or chicken or sprinkled over a salad. You can also use it as a garnish. Coriander is much better used fresh and it's an annual, so is better used up.

Spring Rolls

20–25 frozen spring roll pastry
sheets (approximately
20 cm × 20 cm)
vegetable oil for frying

filling
50 g bean thread vermicelli, soaked
for 15 mins in hot water
200 g pork mince
170 g can of crab meat, well-
drained
⅓ cup cabbage, finely chopped
⅓ cup beanshoots, chopped
2 spring onions, finely chopped
⅓ cup grated carrot
⅓ cup snow peas, finely sliced
1 tbsp chopped coriander
1 tbsp fish sauce
salt and pepper

dipping sauce
1 lime, juiced
1 tbsp brown sugar
1 tbsp fish sauce
3 tbsp water
1 clove garlic, crushed
1 tsp minced or finely chopped hot
chilli
1 tbsp grated carrot
1 tbsp coriander, roughly torn

iceberg lettuce leaves to serve

If I could get myself to Thy Thy in Melbourne's Victoria
Street seven times a week for some of their magnificent
spring rolls, I would! But as I can only manage to do this
occasionally, this is my homemade substitute ...
– Di

1. Allow the spring roll pastry to defrost. Cut each sheet in half.
2. To make the filling, mix all the filling ingredients in a bowl. This mixture
makes about 50 spring rolls, so I often freeze half of the mixture.
3. Wrap 1½ teaspoons of the filling mixture in each half sheet of pastry,
beginning at the bottom of the sheet and folding in the sides as you roll it
up. Wet the top edge of the pastry with a little water to seal the roll.
4. Heat vegetable oil to about 3 cm deep. Fry the rolls in batches of 5–8
(depending on the size of your wok or saucepan). Turn the rolls once in
the oil to allow them to brown evenly. Cook each batch for approximately
3 minutes (or until golden brown and cooked through).
5. To make the dipping sauce, combine the lime juice, brown sugar, fish
sauce, water and garlic. At this point I set some of the sauce aside for the
kids, then I continue to add the chilli, carrot and coriander.
6. Serve the spring rolls with the dipping sauce and iceberg lettuce leaves
for wrapping.

Makes 50 spring rolls

Baked Ricotta Mushrooms

6–8 medium-sized mushrooms
³/₄ cup ricotta cheese
2 slices pancetta, cut into little
  strips
½ small red onion, finely chopped
1 tbsp chopped parsley
½ tbsp chopped dill
1 tbsp lemon juice
cracked pepper
1½ tbsp breadcrumbs
1½ tbsp parmesan, finely grated

Fungi fans are going to love these. You can play around with variations on the herbs and fillings used, and smaller, bite-sized mushies can make yummy canapés. — *Di*

1. Preheat the oven to 200°C.
2. Place the mushrooms on a lined baking tray and remove the stems.
3. Combine the remaining ingredients in a small bowl, keeping the bread-crumbs and parmesan to one side.
4. Fill the mushroom cups with the ricotta mixture.
5. Combine the crumbs and parmesan and sprinkle over the top of the mushrooms.
6. Bake in the preheated oven for 10–15 minutes.

Makes 6–8 mushrooms

Lamb & Coconut Satay

dipping sauce
1 tbsp olive or sesame oil
1 clove crushed garlic
1 tsp finely grated ginger
5 tbsp hoisin sauce
1 tbsp soy sauce
2 tbsp water

meatballs
500 g lamb mince
1 tbsp tomato paste
3 tbsp desiccated coconut
1 tsp ground cumin
3 tbsp lime juice
1 egg
1 tbsp water
2 tbsp finely chopped coriander
1 tbsp finely chopped parsley
  satay sticks (soaked in water
  before use)

While cooking our way through recipes we wanted to use for this book, I happened upon these meatballs. The kids like them, but the adults *really* like them! You may wish to take out the coriander for half the mix if the kids find its taste too strong. If the barbeque is on in summer, whack them on the hotplate. You can make the dipping sauce the day before.
– *Lisa*

1. To make the dipping sauce, fry the garlic and ginger in the oil. Cool slightly, then stir through the remaining ingredients. Refrigerate.
2. For the meatballs, put all the ingredients into a large mixing bowl and combine well.
3. Roll the mixture into small balls and put two or three balls on each satay stick.
4. Grill the skewered meatballs for 4 minutes on each side, or barbeque until cooked through.

Makes 15 satays

Chicken Wings 3 Ways

1½ kg chicken drumettes and
   wingettes
1 tbsp fish sauce
½ cup plain flour
1 tsp ground paprika
1 tsp 'season all' or chicken salt
vegetable oil for frying

Crispy Fried Chicken Wings
A bit naughty but sooooo good!
— *Di*

1. Combine the chicken and fish sauce in a bowl and marinate in the fridge
   for about an hour.
2. Combine all the remaining ingredients in a separate bowl.
3. Once marinated, dust the chicken pieces with the flour mixture.
4. Deep-fry the chicken in batches, in 5 cm of hot oil, for approximately
   8 minutes, or until cooked through and golden brown.

Serves 3–4

marinade
1 cup light soy sauce
2 tbsp olive oil
2 tbsp honey
2 tbsp dry sherry
2 cloves garlic, crushed
2 tsp ground ginger
1 tsp sugar
salt and pepper

12 full chicken wings

My Mum's Marinade
My kids will eat these wings endlessly. This is something I do when I don't want to hear any complaints at dinner time.
— *Di*

1. Preheat the oven to 180°C.
2. Whisk all the marinade ingredients together in a bowl.
3. Add the chicken wings to the marinade, coating them well, and leave
   to marinate for at least half an hour in the fridge.
4. Put the wings in a baking dish and bake in the preheated oven for about
   40 minutes, or until the chicken starts to pull away from the bone.

Serves 3–4

⅓ cup breadcrumbs
⅓ cup sesame seeds
1½ kg chicken drumettes and
  wingettes
½ cup plain flour
1 egg, lightly beaten
olive oil cooking spray

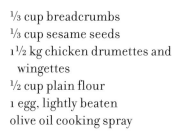

Sesame Crusted Chicken Pieces

My personal favourite.

— *Di*

1. Preheat the oven to 180°C.
2. Combine the breadcrumbs and sesame seeds in a bowl.
3. Dust the chicken in the flour, dip into the egg and then press into the crumb mixture to coat all over.
4. Place the chicken onto a lined baking tray and spray lightly with olive oil.
5. Bake in the preheated oven for around 45 minutes, turning once halfway through the cooking process.

Serves 3–4

'There's a big wide world out there; the possibilities are endless. Let's throw a few things together, hit the road and have an adventure we'll never forget! Maybe we'll stop for a bite along the way...'

Lunchbox Muesli Bars

125 g butter
⅓ cup brown sugar
2 tbsp honey
1 cup oats
½ cup desiccated coconut
½ cup self-raising flour
½ cup dried cranberries
5 chopped up dates
½ cup seeds and nuts such as
    almonds, sunflower seeds,
    cashews, macadamias and pepitas
    (I use a breakfast muesli from the
    health food shop and chop it up in
    the food processor)
⅓ cup tiny choc bits (optional)

Local fundraising cookbooks are a fantastic inspiration for recipes. They usually combine favoured family recipes, sometimes passed down through generations. I adapted this muesli bar slice recipe from one of my school cookbooks to suit my kids' preferences. It does have nuts, so substitute these if you have an intolerant family member.
— *Lisa*

1. Preheat the oven to 180°C.
2. Line a baking tray (23 × 15 cm or similar) with baking paper.
3. Combine the butter, sugar and honey in a saucepan over a medium heat until the sugar has dissolved.
4. Stir in all the remaining ingredients.
5. Transfer the mix to the baking tray and press down with the back of a spoon.
6. Bake for 20 minutes.
7. When cooled, cut into your desired shape—I do fingers bars, or you could do squares or triangles. Keep refrigerated.

Makes 16

Carrot Cake

cake

2 cups plain flour
2 tsp baking powder
1½ tsp bicarbonate of soda
1 tsp salt
2 tsp cinnamon
2 cups raw sugar
1 cup vegetable oil
4 eggs
2 cups grated carrot (about
    1½ medium-sized carrots)
440 g can crushed pineapple,
    drained
½ cup walnuts, finely chopped

cream cheese icing

250 g packet cream cheese,
    softened
30 g butter, softened
1 tsp vanilla essence
250 g icing sugar, sifted
2 tbsp milk

Morning tea at the park? Coffee and cake at your place?
Sounds great; I'll see you there, cake in hand!
— Di

1. Preheat the oven to 180°C.
2. Sift together the dry ingredients for the cake.
3. Add the sugar, oil and eggs and mix, using an electric mixer on low speed.
4. Stir in the carrot, pineapple and nuts.
5. Pour the mixture into a lined cake tin (a large one as this is quite a big cake; alternatively you could make two smaller ones) and bake for about 1 hour.
6. Allow the cake to cool in the tin for 5 minutes before turning onto a wire rack to cool completely before icing.
7. To make the icing, cream together the cheese and butter in an electric mixer.
8. Add the vanilla essence, then gradually stir in the sifted icing sugar and the milk, bit by bit.
9. Spread thickly onto the cooled cake/cakes.

Serves 16

DOUBLING UP

Why not make two cakes from this recipe—one to give away and one to keep at home for the family? A home-baked cake is one of those heartfelt offerings that's always well-received—when welcoming someone to the neighbourhood, as a housewarming gift atop a new platter, or as a great way to return a plate or container with a special touch. These cakes also freeze well: just wrap the cooled cake in foil and pop it away in the freezer for a rainy day.

- Di

Muffins

1 egg
1 cup milk
¾ cup vegetable oil
1¼ cups plain flour
2 tsp baking powder
2 tbsp cocoa
½ cup caster sugar
½ cup oats
1 banana, mashed
12 large chocolate cooking buttons
   (1 per muffin)
muffin papers

Muffins can be really handy for a school lunch box; they're easy to knock up and you can double the mixture and freeze half for afternoon tea sometime, or a weekend snack. When bananas start to look a little tired, I just use them up in a muffin mix. I tend to experiment with different combinations, which keeps it interesting for me. Sometimes I will add orange or lemon zest, a sprinkle of desiccated coconut, raisins or a large handful of frozen berries. Chocolate, oats and banana are the current favourite for the school lunch box in our house. There are plenty of savoury options, too. When you get quick at making them, whip up a batch before school—the house will smell great!

— *Lisa*

1. Preheat the oven to 180°C.
2. Beat together the egg, milk and oil.
3. In a separate bowl, sift and combine the flour, baking powder and cocoa.
4. Add the sifted ingredients, sugar, oats and mashed banana to the egg mix and combine.
5. Pop the muffin papers in a muffin pan and spoon the mixture into them. The muffins will rise, so only half fill the papers.
6. Place a chocolate button on top of each muffin and bake in the oven for 20–25 minutes. When cooked, the tops of the muffins should spring back up when you press them with your finger.

Makes 12 large muffins

BERRIES ON DEMAND
Frozen berries are great to have on hand — I find I use them a lot with the kids. I never use many, but they're nice in smoothies, or for adding to desserts or these muffins.

Lunchbox Pancakes

batter
1 cup plain flour
pinch of salt
1 egg, beaten
1½ cups milk

toppings
jams
cheese, grated
ham or chicken, sliced

Pancakes are usually weekend breakfast fare in our house, but if we have batter left over, we pack them in a school lunch box. They are better cooked up fresh in the morning, but having said that, if time is poor just cook them beforehand and pull them out of the fridge.
– Lisa

1. Sift the flour into a large mixing bowl, then add the salt and egg and combine.
2. Gradually beat the milk into the flour mix.
3. Adjust the mixture to your desired consistency (I prefer thinner pancakes, so usually add a dash more milk).
4. Spray some oil into a non-stick frying pan over a medium heat, then add a ladle of batter, turning the pancakes when bubbles appear on the top and the corners lift easily.
5. For a savoury lunch pancake, layer with thinly sliced ham or chicken and sprinkle with grated cheese or sliced swiss cheese.
6. If packing these up for a morning tea or for the lunch box, use a sweet or savoury spread, or just cheese, then roll the pancake in greaseproof paper and tie it up with string.

Makes 8–10

Pinwheel Sangos

1 loaf unsliced bread, white or
  brown
cream cheese or mayonnaise
ham or egg mix, or another topping
  of your choice
mustards or chutneys according to
  taste

This lunchtime idea feels like a throwback to a '70s cocktail party, but it's something different. You can make a smaller batch, but this version means you can keep some pinwheels for the freezer. You can vary the fillings—even using honey or Vegemite—but it's a good idea to use a cream cheese or mayonnaise to hold the wheel together. Try a sweet version with cream cheese and jam.

— Lisa

1. Remove the crusts from the loaf with a knife. (You can freeze the crusts and use them to make croutons for soup.)
2. Slice the loaf lengthways three or four times according to thickness (each slice should be about 2 cm thick).
3. Use a rolling pin to flatten the bread.
4. Spread each slice with cream cheese or mayonnaise.
5. Next, top with a thin layer of your desired topping.
6. Roll into a wheel, using a little extra cream cheese to 'glue' the end down.
7. Freeze the wheels. (This makes them really easy to cut.)
8. When you're ready to eat, remove the wheels from the freezer and slice. Return any surplus wheels to the freezer.

Makes approximately 20

Double-Decker Finger Sandwiches

3 slices bread per sandwich (you could mix 1 white with 2 brown)
lettuce leaves, rinsed and dried
avocado
chicken, tuna or ham
mayonnaise
cheese, grated or sliced
mustard
curried egg mix (if your kids like it)
carrot, grated or sliced with a peeler
cucumber
spreads (Promite, honey, Vegemite or jam)
tomato
cream cheese
banana, sliced
sultanas

When soggy, uneaten sandwiches start coming home in lunch boxes or are found growing arms and legs in the bottom of a school bag, it's time to come up with a gimmick. The extra effort in preparation will reward you with a happy child post-lunch and less food waste—they could even make these sandwiches themselves the night before. Experiment with different fillings within the layers.
— *Lisa*

1. Start with the bottom layer of brown bread. Top with something like lettuce leaves and avocado.
2. Place the next slice of bread on top and dress with chicken pieces, mayonnaise and grated cheese.
3. Place the final piece of bread on top to finish the deck. Press down.
4. Depending on the bread used, either cut the sandwich or leave it whole. You can remove any crusts for a pretty effect—cream cheese and jam deckers look nice with no crusts.

Wraps

Mountain Bread or soft tortilla
  wrap
mayonnaise, chutney or mustard
lettuce
cheese (I like camembert for mine)
chicken, turkey, ham, tuna or
salami
beansprouts
carrot, grated
cucumber, thinly sliced
avocado
beetroot

Wraps are the ultimate lunch box winner for my kids.
If I give them a choice, mountain bread wraps are their
pick. They all vary in their individual tastes, but I don't
care as long as they eat it. A great vegetarian option,
wraps hold a good amount, and if you wrap them well
bits don't drip and fall out.
— Lisa

1. Lay out the required number of wraps on top of individual pieces of
   greaseproof paper—the paper should be just big enough to create a handle
   for the wrap.
2. Spread chutney, mayonnaise or mustard on each wrap.
3. Favouring the right side of the wrap, place your fillings.
4. Roll each wrap quite tightly, then re-roll it in the set-up paper. If you
   position the wrap an inch above the bottom of the paper, you can tuck the
   bottom under mid-roll so that nothing falls out.
5. Use string to tie the paper around the wrap.

```
SUSHI ROLLS
Sushi rolls are great for school lunches. You may
be lucky enough to have a Japanese takeaway nearby,
but if not, have a go at making them yourself. The
bigger supermarkets carry most of the ingredients
needed, even the sushi mats for rolling. Make sure
you use sushi rice, and try the Japanese mayonnaise
- it's really tasty. Sushi rolls are fiddly to make
when you first start, but after a few attempts you
will show significant improvement. Personally, I
cheat. A friend put me onto a sushi maker, which is
great. I found it at a kitchen supply store and the
kids actually want to make the sushi themselves!
```

Zucchini Slice

2 medium-sized zucchini, grated
1 cup cheddar cheese, grated
1 onion, grated
1 cup self-raising flour
½ cup vegetable oil
5 eggs, lightly beaten
4 middle bacon rashers, chopped
   into 1 cm squares
2 tbsp dill leaves, chopped
salt and pepper

The zucchini slice is something new for the kids' lunch boxes and a great picnic basket addition. This slice is easy to eat and a meal in itself; try it without bacon as a vegetarian option.
— *Di*

1. Preheat the oven to 180°C.
2. Combine all the ingredients in a large bowl and stir well.
3. Grease a 20 cm × 30 cm baking dish. Pour the mixture into the dish and spread evenly.
4. Bake in the oven for 45 minutes, or until golden and firm to the touch.
5. Serve warm or cold.

Makes 9–12 pieces

ORGANISING THE PAPER TRAIL
When kids start at kindergarten and school, there is a significant paperwork trail that follows: timetables, contact lists, book lists, uniform lists, excursion information, notes to sign and return, party invitations ... the list goes on. To contain it all, a few years ago my partner created a lever-arch file divided into sections. It's a simple solution and it works since everything can be found in the one spot. My other lifesaver is the family calendar. It's a month-by-month planner and everyone's names are on there, so we can all see what's coming up at a glance-appointments, school duties, parties, project due dates ... just make sure you write it on the calendar as soon as it comes through the door.

ready set go
are we there yet?

The family road trip, no matter what the distance,
can be far better endured and enjoyed the more
organised you are before you back out of the
driveway. Even just the one hour journey to Trishy
and Grumps' place (my kids' grandparents) requires
several standard operating procedures to occur
before we head off.

- A small bag of spare clothing items can be a handy
  fixture in the boot of your car at all times. You'll
  need to give it an annual update (as children tend
  to grow like grass) but a dry top, for example,
  can mean the difference between a full day of fun
  or having to abort your mission and go home early
  with a cold, grizzly kid.

- Tissues and wet wipes are standard ... don't EVER leave home without them! I like to include an old tea towel as it's useful for a wide range of things, including drying off a slide or swing on a damp day at the park.

- A rubbish bag is a good addition, especially if there's food involved, or someone with a head cold!

- If the trip is long enough and there are snacks to share, bring along some cups to decant things like popcorn, chips and rice crackers. It's neater than everyone trying to grab a handful, and saves the mess of a torn bag. This is also a handy idea at the park or beach.

- My personal favourite, and regular lifesaving device, is the salad crisper with lid. For any family with someone that suffers from car sickness (us included), this is a ripper idea. It's the perfect size and shape for the job, and having a fitted lid means that unpleasant odours can be held at bay whilst the driver can find a safe spot to pull over. Wash or wipe out the bowl, then continue on your merry way!

- Portable DVD players or DS-style game units are handy on long trips if you have access to them. Alternatively, you can seize this opportunity for some quality family time and communication. Games like 'I Spy' can get everybody involved, and if some kids are too young to play by naming a letter (e.g. 'I spy, with my little eye, something beginning with S') then play by naming a colour (e.g. 'I spy, with my little eye, something that is blue'). The 'Shopping Game' is another simple and fun game for everyone to play. One person starts with the line 'I went to the market and I bought a ... watermelon' (for example). The next person says, 'I went to the market and I bought a watermelon and ... some socks' (for example). Each person takes it in turn to add something to the list of items bought at the market after first having to recall all the previous items. See how long your list can get!

- There's no doubt that sometimes we all need a bit of shush in a confined space, and a little treat like a Chupa Chup or some patty pan toffee (see recipe in our Celebrate section) can provide a decent period of relief.

Hawaiian- & Supreme-Style Pizza Scrolls

2 cups self-raising flour, sifted
1 tbsp caster sugar
30 g butter at room temperature
¾ cup milk
2 tbsp tomato paste
½ cup ham, shaved and cut into thin strips
½ cup mild salami, shaved and cut into thin strips
¾ cup pineapple pieces, drained
⅓ green capsicum, finely sliced
1 large mushroom, finely sliced
1½ cups grated mozzarella cheese

We all know that kids love pizza, and some would eat it for lunch every day if we let them! With these home-made savoury scrolls, you can send your troops off knowing that they're eating the freshest of ingredients. Make up a batch using these, or your own favourite toppings, and freeze them individually … hey presto, school lunches done for a week!

— Di

1. Preheat the oven to 180°C.
2. Place the sifted flour and the sugar in a bowl. Chop the butter, add it to the bowl and rub it into the flour mixture until it resembles bread-crumbs.
3. Stir in the milk and mix to form a dough.
4. Place the dough on a floured surface and knead lightly. Using a rolling pin, roll the dough out to roughly 30 cm × 40 cm wide to make the pizza base.
5. Spread the base with the tomato paste. Sprinkle ham on one half of the 40 cm width and salami on the other. Top the ham side with pineapple and the salami section with capsicum and mushroom slices. Sprinkle mozzarella over the lot.
6. Starting at the bottom of the pizza base, roll the dough firmly upwards to make a 40 cm long roll. Use a serrated knife to cut the roll into 12 even slices.
7. Arrange the slices on a greased baking tray (about 20 cm × 30 cm) so they are sitting connected to each other and in a single layer. Bake in the oven for 30 minutes, or until browned.
8. Serve warm or cold.

Serves 12

(Very) Special Fried Rice

1 cup rice
2 rashers middle bacon
2 eggs
2 tbsp milk
½ cup peas (fresh or frozen)
2 tbsp vegetable oil
¼ cup light soy sauce
½ cup shredded barbeque chicken (optional—I only add this if I happen to have some leftover chicken in the fridge)
½ cup small cooked prawns
2 spring onions, finely sliced

Mmmm … I love fried rice. Whether it's hot or cold, for breakfast, lunch or dinner, from a china bowl or a paper carton, a plastic container or straight from the pan, it's all good! When I grew up it was always the side dish to my mum's delicious chicken wings (see recipe in Snack section). I use white Basmati rice, but brown rice can be used as an alternative. It's also worth noting that I use the same frying pan throughout the whole cooking process.
— *Di*

1. Cook the rice as per packet instructions, then spread it out on a tray or large baking dish and refrigerate for at least an hour.
2. Chop the bacon, cook in a frying pan or wok and set aside.
3. Whisk the eggs and milk together and cook (in the same pan you used for the bacon—it should be left greased, ready for the egg) as a thin omelette in the pan. Roughly chop the omelette into strips with a spatula before setting aside.
4. Blanch the peas and set aside.
5. On a medium heat, add the vegetable oil to the wok or frying pan and fry the rice for a couple of minutes. Add the soy sauce and mix it through the rice evenly.
6. Lower the heat and add the bacon, egg, peas, chicken, prawns and spring onions. Turn the rice with a large spoon to distribute all the ingredients and to heat them through.

Serves 4 as a meal; 6–8 as a side dish

'The secret of happiness is not doing what one likes, but in liking what one does.'
—J. M. Barrie

Traffic Light Pasta Salad with Salami

3 cups dry pasta (I use orecchiette)
½ cup whole egg mayonnaise
1 tsp wholegrain mustard
1 tbsp parsley, finely chopped
salt and pepper
½ cup green beans, chopped into
  5 mm pieces
½ cup yellow capsicum, finely
  diced
1 cup cherry tomatoes, halved or
  quartered depending on their size
5 thin mild salami slices, cut into
  1 cm strips
⅓ cup parmesan, finely grated

I love this salad, and the great news is, so do the kids! It's colourful, with a little bit of crunch, and hearty enough to be called lunch all on its own. Pack it up in a well-sealed container and off you go. Different pasta shapes can give this salad a new twist each time you make it. It's a definite green light …
— Di

1. Cook the pasta according to the packet instructions, drain under cold running water and then pop it in the fridge to cool it completely.
2. Combine the mayonnaise, mustard, parsley and salt and pepper in a small bowl to make a dressing.
3. Stir the dressing through the cooled pasta.
4. Add the chopped beans, capsicum, tomatoes and salami. Finally, gently stir through the parmesan.
5. Keep this salad refrigerated before sending it packing with a freezer brick.

Serves 6-8

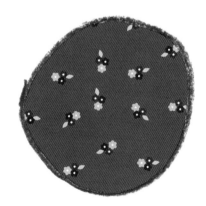
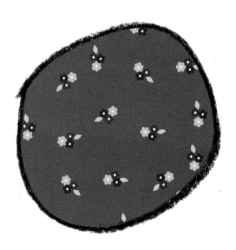

LUNCH BOX LOGISTICS

Keeping lunches fresh impacts on whether they get eaten. Over the years I've amassed an array of containers in different sizes and shapes for school lunch boxes and travelling, and find I use them all for different applications. (Half the lids don't come back-lost in the plastic vortex every school has — so I buy the same brand to try and match up.) There are little containers for fruit or dried fruit to snack on, and round containers for holding hummus and vegie sticks. An insulated lunch box or iceblock lunch box is also helpful in keeping food cool, particularly in the summer. A good drinks container is also a must — I prefer the aluminium ones over the plastic versions for carrying water to school. When the kids are old enough, there are some well-made glass bottles available. I always carry one.

Chicken Salad

3 middle bacon rashers, chopped
   roughly into 2 cm strips
½ store-bought barbeque chicken,
   cooled and roughly shredded
1 small red onion, finely diced
1 small red capsicum, diced
1 handful chives, chopped
2 tbsp whole egg mayonnaise
cracked pepper
baby cos lettuce leaves
balsamic vinegar

crusty bread to serve

This simple recipe was passed on to me by a work colleague years ago and has proven to be useful time and time again. A yummy chicken mix is a really versatile meal to have up your sleeve, and with these simple ingredients you can quickly create an entree or main, sandwich filling or wrap. It's an easy and economical way to make use of yesterday's leftover roast chook, and just half a chicken can serve up to four people as a main course.

— *Di*

1. Fry the bacon bits until crispy, then set aside to cool.
2. Mix together the shredded chicken, onion, capsicum, chives and mayonnaise, along with some cracked pepper. Add the bacon bits just before serving to keep them crisp.
3. Arrange the lettuce leaves on each plate and drizzle with balsamic vinegar (about 1 teaspoon per plate). Place a generous mound of chicken onto the dressed leaves.
4. Serve with crusty bread.

Serves 4

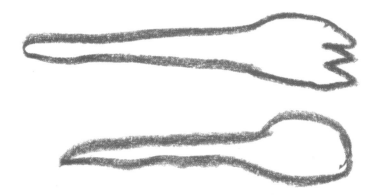

'How was your day? School fun? Busy at work? There's lots to tell each other while we enjoy this meal together, so bring along a big appetite and your loveliest manners please ... Hey, guess what?!'

3

feast ★

Ham Hock Minestrone with Pasta Scraps

10 cups water
1 ham hock
2 bay leaves
1 beef stock cube, dissolved in
  ¼ cup boiling water
2 celery sticks, chopped
1 carrot, diced
1 parsnip, diced
1 zucchini, diced
1 small pumpkin wedge, diced
2 garlic cloves, finely chopped
1 × 140 g tub tomato paste
salt and pepper
1 × 125 g can red kidney beans,
  drained
½ cup pasta, crushed
½ cup parsley, chopped

Time for a kitchen tidy up? Grab your favourite stock-pot or the slow cooker, gather up all those little scraps and leftovers, and create a hearty meal with the lot!
— *Di*

1. Place the ham hock in a large pot with the water, bay leaves and stock. Bring to the boil and then lower the heat to a simmer and cover with a lid.
2. Meanwhile, chop all your vegies into fairly even-sized pieces and be sure to give the crisper a good clean out in the process. The vegetables I've listed for this recipe are a guide only and just about anything can be chopped up and tossed into this soup.
3. Add the garlic, vegetables, tomato paste and seasoning to the pot and simmer, covered, for at least 1 hour 30 minutes.
4. Remove the ham hock from the pot and discard the fat and bone. Shred the meat and return it to the pot.
5. Add the beans and the pasta. This is another opportunity to use up the last few strands of spaghetti in the jar and/or several bow ties, spirals or whatever you have in little packets throughout the shelves—just crush it up and throw it in. Simmer the soup for a further 30 minutes before serving, sprinkled with parsley.

Serves 6

Chicken & Sweetcorn Soup

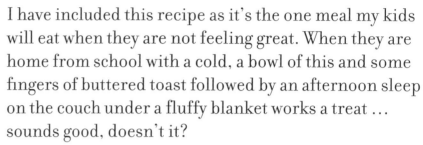

1 tbsp olive oil
1 brown onion, finely chopped
2 chicken breasts, cut into strips
1.5 litres chicken stock (hot)
420 g can creamed corn
    cornflour to thicken

I have included this recipe as it's the one meal my kids will eat when they are not feeling great. When they are home from school with a cold, a bowl of this and some fingers of buttered toast followed by an afternoon sleep on the couch under a fluffy blanket works a treat … sounds good, doesn't it?
— Lisa

1. In a heavy-based pot, sauté the onion in the olive oil.
2. Add all the other ingredients to the pot, except for the cornflour, and bring to the boil.
3. Turn down the heat and simmer, uncovered, for 45 minutes.
4. If you prefer a thicker consistency, sprinkle in a tablespoon of cornflour.

Serves 4

Speedy Thai Beef Salad

marinade

¼ cup light soy sauce

juice of 1 lime

2 tbsp fish sauce

1 garlic clove, crushed

1 tsp hot chilli paste (lessen or eliminate for young kids' tastes)

1 tbsp brown sugar

½ cup torn coriander leaves (lessen or eliminate for young kids' tastes)

2 porterhouse steaks, thick cut (approx. 250 g per adult)

garnish (optional)

1 small chilli, finely sliced
    extra coriander leaves

Here's a quick and flavoursome meal that's easily adapted to suit everyone's tastes.
— *Di*

1. Combine the marinade ingredients in a large bowl.
2. Cook the steak over a high heat on a barbeque or griddle pan so that the meat is rare. This should take about 2–3 minutes per side. Rest for a few minutes before slicing thinly with a sharp knife and adding to the marinade.
3. Toss the meat in the marinade, coating it well, and leave for a couple of minutes.
4. Serve on a bed of creamy mashed potatoes (see recipe p. 110), drizzle with some extra marinade and sprinkle with fresh chilli and coriander leaves.

Serves 2

Personalised Pasties

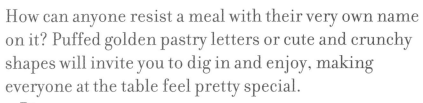

400 g premium minced beef
1 onion, diced
1 carrot, diced
1 zucchini, diced
1 parsnip, diced
1 red capsicum, diced
100 g green beans, sliced
    into 5 mm pieces
1 cup parsley, chopped
salt and pepper
8 frozen puff pastry sheets
1 egg, lightly beaten

How can anyone resist a meal with their very own name
on it? Puffed golden pastry letters or cute and crunchy
shapes will invite you to dig in and enjoy, making
everyone at the table feel pretty special.
— *Di*

1. Preheat the oven to 160°C.
2. Combine the beef, chopped vegetables, parsley and seasoning in a large
   bowl, using your hands to mix thoroughly.
3. Place about one-sixth to one-eighth of the mixture onto the bottom half
   of a defrosted puff pastry sheet and fold over to enclose, pressing around
   the edges with a fork to seal. I use a full sheet for an adult serve, but you
   can cut sheets to suit various appetites.
4. Cut letters or a simple shapes, message or design out of pastry off-cuts.
   Lay these on top of your pasties before pricking them with a fork.
5. Arrange the pasties on lined baking trays and brush with the beaten egg.
6. Bake in the oven for around 45 minutes, or until the pastry is puffed and
   golden brown.
7. Serve with plenty of tomato sauce.

Makes 6–8 large, or up to 16 half-size pasties

'A mother's arms are made
of tenderness and children
sleep soundly in them.'
—Victor Hugo

Chicken & Leek Parcels

filling
1 tbsp butter
1 tbsp olive oil
2 leeks, sliced
1¼ kg chicken thigh fillets, roughly
　chopped into 3 cm pieces
½ cup chicken stock
½ cup thickened cream
2 tbsp cornflour mixed into
　¼ cup water
8 asparagus spears, chopped into
　2 cm lengths
1 small bunch chives, chopped
salt and pepper
5 frozen puff pastry sheets
1 egg, lightly beaten

I love pies of any description, and this is one of my favourites. I regularly make large quantities of these in various sizes to suit different family members, and keep them frozen for a quick and easy option at the end of those busier days.
— *Di*

1. Preheat the oven to 180°C.
2. Heat the butter and the oil in a frying pan. Add the leeks to the pan and soften. Remove the leeks from the pan and set aside.
3. In the same frying pan, heat a dash more oil and seal the chicken pieces in batches over a high heat (this takes about 2 minutes for each batch).
4. Return the chicken and leeks to the pan and add the chicken stock. Simmer gently for 5 minutes.
5. While on a low heat, stir through the cream and then the cornflour mixture until the sauce thickens. Turn the heat off and allow the mixture to cool slightly.
6. Stir through the asparagus, chives and seasoning. Leave the mixture to cool.
7. Take the pastry sheets out of the freezer. Pile spoonfuls of the cooled chicken mixture onto the bottom half of each defrosted pastry sheet. Fold the pastry over the chicken and press the edges together to seal the parcel. Use a full sheet for each adult serve.
8. Prick the parcels with a fork, then brush with the egg. Bake on a lined tray in the oven for about 40 minutes, or until puffed and golden brown.

Makes 5 adult-sized parcels

Chicken Tacos

1 tbsp olive oil
1 brown onion, finely chopped
500 g chicken mince
½ cup water
1 sachet Mexican seasoning (you
   can get this at the supermarket)
2 tomatoes, diced
2 cups grated cheese
½ iceberg lettuce, shredded
1 avocado
1 tsp lemon juice (optional)
sour cream
salsa (see recipe for homemade
   salsa on p. 28)
taco shells (at least 10)

Tacos are a quick, sure-fire dinner for a busy family. With tacos you can roll out dinner as you need it, which is perfect when everyone is operating on different schedules. Tacos are both colourful and healthy, and the kids have a great time assembling their own.
– Lisa

1. Heat the oil over a medium heat in a heavy-based saucepan.
2. Add the onion to the pan and cook until softened.
3. Add the chicken mince to the onion and brown the meat.
4. Add the water and seasoning to the pan, then reduce the heat to a simmer for 25 minutes, stirring now and then to prevent the mixture from sticking. Add extra water if necessary.
5. Meanwhile, place the diced tomatoes, grated cheese and sliced lettuce in separate serving dishes.
6. In a bowl, mash the avocado with a fork and add lemon juice if desired.
7. Place the sour cream and salsa in serving bowls.
8. Heat the taco shells according to the packet instructions.
9. Transfer the chicken mince to a serving dish.
10. Put all the ingredients out on the table and let the customers do the rest.

Serves 4

Pot Pies

filling
500 g diced beef
1 cup plain flour, seasoned
2 tbsp olive oil
1 brown onion, diced
1 garlic clove, crushed
400 g can crushed tomatoes
2 cups beef stock
sprinkle of mixed herbs
1 carrot, diced
1 large potato, cut into 1 cm cubes
½ cup peas

8 ramekin bowls
2 sheets frozen shortcrust pastry
2 tbsp milk

These little individual beef and vegetable pot pies are a real treat on a cold winter's night, or for a family lunch at the weekend.

— *Lisa*

1. Preheat the oven to 180°C.
2. Coat the diced beef in the seasoned flour.
3. Heat the olive oil in a pan and brown the diced beef in batches, then remove and set aside.
4. Sauté the onion and garlic in the pan until softened.
5. Return the beef to the pan. Add the tomatoes, stock and herbs and simmer on a low heat for 1 hour.
6. Add the diced carrot, potato and peas to the pan and continue to simmer for a further hour, or until the beef is tender.
7. Place the cooked stew in individual ramekins and top each bowl with a cover of defrosted shortcrust pastry. Trim the pastry to the size of each ramekin and pinch around the edge to seal. You could use any leftover pastry to decorate the pies by using a cookie cutter shape.
8. With a pastry brush, brush the top of the pies with the milk.
9. Place the ramekins in the oven and bake for 20 minutes.

Makes 8 pies

Spanakopita Coil

filling
160 g spinach leaves
350 g feta cheese, crumbled
250 g ricotta cheese
150 g cheddar cheese, grated
3 eggs
½ cup parsley, chopped
½ tsp ground nutmeg
salt and pepper

pastry
50 g butter, melted
1 tbsp olive oil
375 g pack filo pastry
1 tbsp sesame seeds

If three cheeses and layers of buttery, flaky pastry is the only way you'll witness your kids eating spinach, then I say it's worth it! There's no denying the sense of satisfaction (and perhaps a little victory) as they tuck into what I simply refer to as 'cheese pie'. Popeye would be proud.

— *Di*

1. Preheat the oven to 180°C.
2. Wash the spinach in a colander, then run a kettle of boiling water over the leaves to wilt them. Squeeze out the juices and finely chop the leaves.
3. Combine all the filling ingredients in a bowl, mixing with a fork or your hands to ensure that no large chunks of feta remain.
4. Prepare the pastry, melt the butter with a splash of oil. Using a pastry brush, grease a round baking dish approximately 25 cm in diameter.
5. Lay out a sheet of pastry horizontally and brush it all over with the butter mixture. Place another sheet of pastry directly on top. Put a row of the cheese and spinach mixture across the bottom of the pastry (about 2 cm from the edge) and roll upwards to make a long sausage shape, trimming off the last 5 cm of pastry at the top edge. Place the 'sausage' against the outer edge of your circular dish, seam down.
6. Repeat the process and connect each 'sausage' onto the end of the last, winding towards the centre of the dish. Don't pack the dish too tightly—it takes about four lengths to fill this size dish.
7. Brush the top of the pie with the remaining butter mixture and sprinkle with the sesame seeds. Bake in the preheated oven for around 40 minutes, or until golden brown.

Serves 4–6

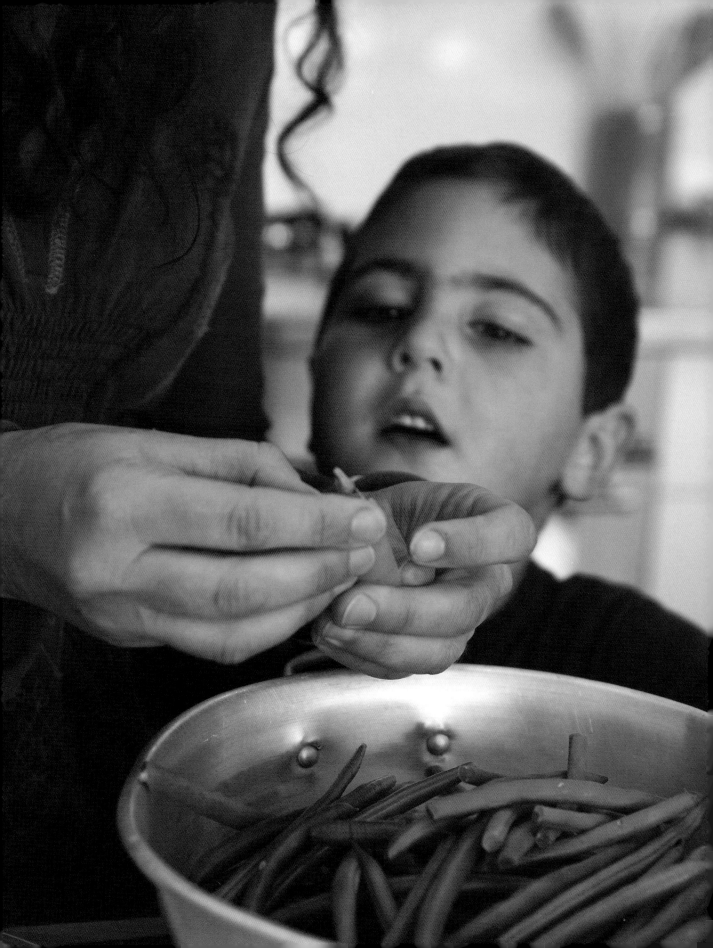

'Small cheer, and great welcome makes a merry feast.'
—William Shakespeare

Beetroot Risotto

1 beetroot, peeled and diced
2 beetroots, grated or juiced
1 litre beef stock
2 tbsp olive oil
1 leek, finely chopped
½ Spanish onion, finely chopped
1 clove garlic, crushed
2 tbsp butter
2 cups arborio rice
1 cup orange juice
1 cup red wine
2 tbsp tomato ketchup
¼ cup grated parmesan cheese
   parmesan shavings to finish

I have always been a fanatical risotto lover. The best I ever had was a beetroot and bocconcini risotto at Tolarno in St Kilda in 1998 (last century). Bright pink, with stretchy bocconcini cheese in every bite, I have never forgotten that risotto experience. A good stock is essential for a successful risotto, and try not to overcook the arborio—I prefer the rice to be slightly crunchy. Risotto is a little time intensive as you can't walk away from the stove, but it's a good way to use up leftovers from the fridge. This recipe has a little red wine in it; if you'd rather not include it, add an extra cup of stock.
— *Lisa*

1. Put the diced beetroot on a lined baking tray and bake in a preheated oven at 180°C for approximately 20 minutes, until cooked.
2. Grate or juice the remaining two beetroots.
3. Put the beef stock in a saucepan on the back of the stove and keep warm.
4. In a heavy-based pan, heat the olive oil and cook the leek, onion and garlic for 2 minutes until softened.
5. Add 1 tablespoon of the butter to the pan, then mix in the arborio rice and stir to coat the rice.
6. Add the orange juice and wine, stir through, and then add the grated beetroot and the tomato ketchup.
7. Start adding the warm stock, a cup at a time, stirring the risotto all the while so that it does not stick.
8. When all the stock has been used, check the rice consistency. If it is not cooked, add some more liquid. The risotto should be creamy and the rice just a little crunchy.
9. Stir in the remaining tablespoon of butter and the grated parmesan.
10. Spoon into bowls and garnish with the parmesan shavings.

Serves 4–6

Spaghetti Bolognese

2 tbsp olive oil
1 leek, rinsed and diced
1 clove garlic, crushed
1 carrot, diced
1 stalk celery, finely sliced
500 g minced beef
1 can diced tomatoes *or*
3 tomatoes, skinned, deseeded
  and chopped
400 ml beef stock
2 tbsp chopped basil leaves
1 bay leaf
⅓ cup tomato sauce
⅓ cup peas
500 g fresh spaghetti
⅓ cup chopped fresh parsley
1 cup grated parmesan cheese

Everyone has a version of spaghetti bolognese—this one just offers up a variation on the theme. We were out one night for dinner with the kids and they had this bolognese and loved it so much I asked what was in it. Tomato sauce was the secret weapon ... it was also pureed slightly to give it a smoother texture (which gives me the opportunity to hide some more vegetables!). I also think the fresh spaghetti is a winner.

— Lisa

1. In a heavy-based pan, sauté the leek and garlic in the olive oil. After 2 minutes, add the carrot and celery and cook for a further 2 minutes.
2. Add the mince to the pan and fry until brown.
3. Add the tomatoes, stock, basil leaves and bay leaf. Simmer for 50 minutes, uncovered, to reduce the volume of liquid.
4. Add the tomato ketchup and peas and simmer for a further 10 minutes.
5. Remove the bay leaf from the sauce and, using a hand blender, puree slightly to a smoother sauce.
6. Serve with lightly buttered fresh spaghetti, finely grated parmesan and parsley (for those who like it).

Serves 4

LEFTOVERS
We usually double this recipe
so we can store a frozen meal.
Any leftovers are always good in
a toasted jaffle, or simply on
toast. See notes on pp. 96-8 for
tips on buying fresh pasta.

pasta

Pasta is one of the most popular foods in the world. Like rice, its versatility affords it this honour. You can buy pasta dried or fresh, or try making it yourself.

— Lisa

Suggested Serves For Pasta
Ann and Nellie McWaters from The Pasta Eater suggest
the following quantities when buying pasta:

fresh plain pasta	stuffed pasta	dried pasta
adult 150g/head	adult 200g/head	adult 115g/head
child 75g/head	child 120g/head	child 60g/head

Always add sea salt to your pan of boiling water
before adding the pasta.

Long Pasta

Spaghetti
Spaghetti is the most common of pastas, ranging
in thickness from vermicelli to spaghettoni. It
is available fresh or dried.

Linguine
Linguine is a flattened spaghetti. In Italian, it
means 'little tongues'. It is available fresh or
dried.

Tagliatelle
Tagliatelle, or what the Romans call fettuccine
(slightly thinner), are long, flat ribbon noodles.
It is available fresh or dried.

Pappardelle
Wider than a tagliatelle and with a smooth, silky texture, pappardelle is a good pasta to serve with dishes that have thick sauces, like a ragout or stroganoff.

Lasagne
Lasagne are flat sheets of pasta. They are available fresh, dried or as easy-cook versions, which are used dry, straight from the packaging.

Short pasta

Farfalle
Farfalle means butterflies, but they look more like bow ties.

Fusilli
Fusilli are spirals of thin pasta that look like springs.

Maccheroni
Maccheroni are hollow-shaped pasta which are terrific for adding to soups. They are available in longer lengths, but the short are more popular.

Conchiglie
Conchiglie are the shell- (conch-) shaped pasta. The shape of the pasta traps the sauce. Conchiglie are available in different sizes.

Penne
Penne are hollow tubes with ridges and diagonally cut ends. Penne are available in different sizes.

Rigatoni
Rigatoni are thick, hollow, ridged pasta tubes and are slightly chewy in texture.

Orecchiette
Orecchiette means 'little ears'. These small, bowl-shaped pasta are slightly chewy in texture.

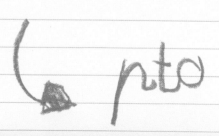

pto

stuffed pasta

There are so many stuffings for pasta, including ricotta, spinach, meat, pumpkin, or even lobster. My favourite is a pumpkin tortellini with burnt sage butter.

Cannelloni
Cannelloni are rolls of pasta, which carry a stuffing inside. They are baked in the oven.

Agnolotti
Agnolotti are little pasta pockets, half-moon shaped.

Tortellini
Tortellini means 'little pies'. They are a ring-shaped, stuffed pasta.

Ravioli
Ravioli are generally square-shaped stuffed pasta. However, the shapes can vary from oblong to small ovals to large squares. The distinctive rippled edging is what identifies it.

other pastas

Gnocchi
Gnocchi is made from potatoes and flour. It is a chewier pasta, not unlike a mini dumpling.

Cous Cous
Cous cous is a grain-like pasta usually served under meat or in salads. It can be eaten hot or cold.

Orzo
Orzo is a small, rice-shaped pasta often used in soups. (Risi is a smaller version of orzo.)

Seafood Pasta

500 g spaghetti
50 g butter
1 tbsp olive oil
1 garlic clove, crushed
1 cup raw prawns, medium-sized
and shelled
1 cup firm fish like gummy flake,
diced
¼ cup lemon juice
⅓ cup parsley, chopped
2 spring onions, finely sliced

Twirly whirly fun! The family will love these simple flavours, and it's an easy way to introduce an extra serve of fish into the mealtime repertoire.
— *Di*

1. Cook the spaghetti as per instructions on the pack.
2. Meanwhile, heat the butter and oil in a pan and lightly fry the garlic. Add the seafood and cook for a couple of minutes until the prawns turn orange in colour. Add the lemon juice and turn off the heat.
3. Drain the spaghetti, then add it to the seafood pan along with the parsley and spring onions, tossing gently to combine.
4. Serve in pasta bowls and drizzle with leftover pan juices.

Serves 4

Carbonara Gnocchi Bake

4 middle bacon rashers, roughly
  chopped
3 medium-sized mushrooms,
  sliced
2 garlic cloves, crushed
2 tbsp olive oil
1 egg
⅔ cup thickened cream
1 cup cheddar cheese, grated
½ tsp nutmeg
cracked pepper
500 g bag of gnocchi
2 spring onions, finely sliced
2 tbsp parsley, chopped
¼ cup parmesan cheese, grated

These comforting little dishes of deliciousness will put
a smile on everyone's face!
– Di

1. Preheat the oven to 200°C.
2. Sauté the bacon, mushrooms and garlic in the oil over a medium heat for
   about 5 minutes.
3. Lightly whisk the egg, cream, cheddar cheese, nutmeg and pepper
   together in a bowl.
4. Cook the gnocchi in boiling salted water until it floats. Drain and tip into
   the bowl of egg mixture. Toss to combine, then add the fried ingredients,
   spring onions and parsley.
5. Spoon into individual ramekins and sprinkle with the grated parmesan.
   Bake in the preheated oven for around 10 minutes, or until the cheese
   has browned.

Serves 4

Pastitsio

meat sauce
3 tbsp olive oil
25 g butter
1 large onion, diced
1 garlic clove, crushed
600 g mince beef
1 × 400 g can diced tomatoes
2 tbsp tomato paste
1 cup water
½ cup red wine
2 bay leaves
½ tsp oregano
salt and pepper

1 × 400 g packet tubular spaghetti

béchamel sauce
250 g butter
1¼ cups self-raising flour
5 cups milk
2 eggs
½ cup parmesan cheese, grated

topping
1 egg, lightly beaten
2 tbsp parmesan cheese, finely
  grated

I cook this meal a lot at home and it differs each time. I usually add some vegies into the meat sauce and sometimes I make it with various types of noodles, but no matter what I do, it never tastes as good as when Mum makes it! And now that I have her recipe, I know why … I have a sneaking suspicion it has something to do with the butter content in the béchamel sauce … Wow! Anyway, this is her version, passed down from my great grandmother. It makes a huge tray and would easily feed ten people, but I usually make two meals with this quantity and freeze one of them for later.
— Di

1. Preheat the oven to 180°C.
2. In a large frying pan, heat the oil and butter and soften the onion. Add the garlic, then push the onions and garlic to the side of the pan and increase the heat. Add the mince to the pan and brown over a high heat, then stir the onions through the meat.
3. Add the remaining meat sauce ingredients to the pan, stir well to combine, then cover and reduce the heat to a simmer for at least an hour.
4. Meanwhile, cook the spaghetti in rapidly boiling salted water as per the packet instructions. Drain well and set aside.
5. To make your béchamel sauce, melt the butter in a large saucepan, then stir in the flour, being careful not to let it brown. When the flour is mixed through, add half the milk and whisk quickly. Use a wooden spoon to scrape the corners of the saucepan regularly. When the sauce thickens again, add the remaining milk and continue to whisk.

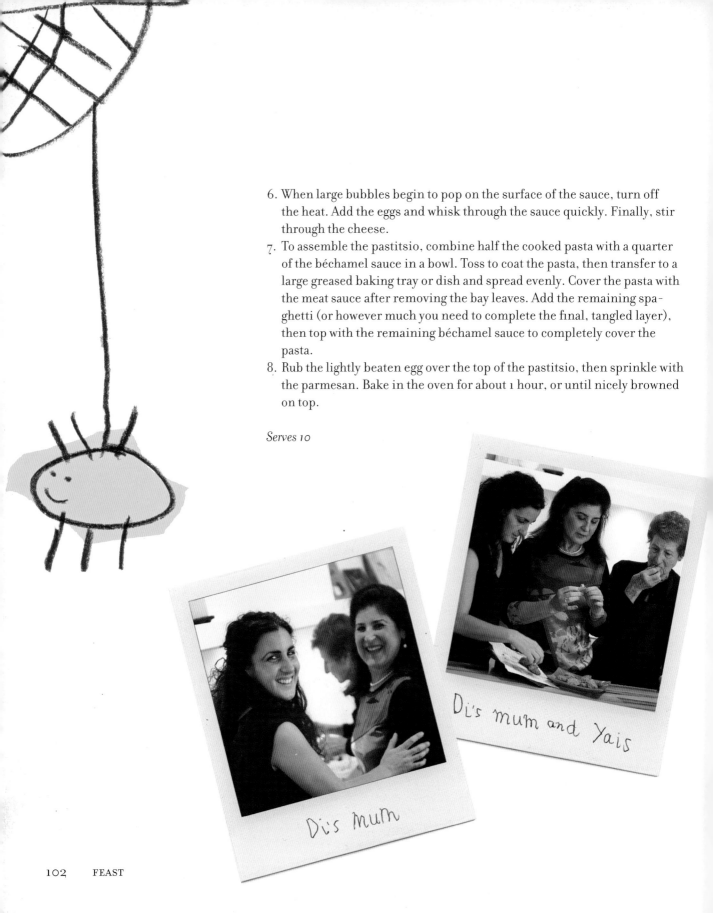

6. When large bubbles begin to pop on the surface of the sauce, turn off the heat. Add the eggs and whisk through the sauce quickly. Finally, stir through the cheese.

7. To assemble the pastitsio, combine half the cooked pasta with a quarter of the béchamel sauce in a bowl. Toss to coat the pasta, then transfer to a large greased baking tray or dish and spread evenly. Cover the pasta with the meat sauce after removing the bay leaves. Add the remaining spaghetti (or however much you need to complete the final, tangled layer), then top with the remaining béchamel sauce to completely cover the pasta.

8. Rub the lightly beaten egg over the top of the pastitsio, then sprinkle with the parmesan. Bake in the oven for about 1 hour, or until nicely browned on top.

Serves 10

Di's mum

Di's mum and Yais

Chicken Parmas

6 chicken fillets or thighs (I prefer thighs)
1 cup plain flour
2 eggs, lightly beaten with a dash of milk
1 cup breadcrumbs
3 tbsp olive oil
20 g butter

topping
olive oil
1 onion, finely diced
1 garlic clove, crushed
1 can crushed tomatoes
salt and pepper
1 tbsp torn basil leaves
8 slices ham off the bone
100 g cheddar cheese, sliced

This is a definite family favourite at our house—most like it with the lot, while some prefer to skip the tomato layer. Whichever way it goes to the table, there's never a scrap left on anyone's plate.
— *Di*

1. Crumb the chicken by dusting it with the flour, then soaking in the egg wash and pressing into the breadcrumbs.
2. Now make the sauce. In a small saucepan, soften the onion and garlic in a dash of olive oil, then tip in the tomatoes and cook on a medium heat for a few minutes. Season with salt and pepper and add the torn basil leaves. Turn off the heat.
3. Heat the 3 tablespoons of olive oil and the butter in a large pan and fry the crumbed chicken until cooked through and golden on both sides.
4. Transfer the cooked fillets to a lined baking tray and cover each schnitzel with a slice of ham. Top with a couple of spoonfuls of tomato mixture, then cover with the cheese slices.
5. Put the baking tray under a hot grill until the cheese melts and begins to brown. Serve the parmas with hand-cut chips (see recipe p. 120), a green salad and a pot for the adults—pub style!

Serves 6

Chicken Curry with Coconut

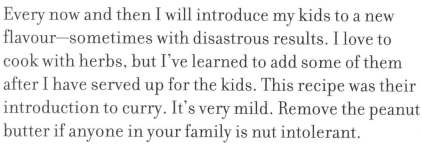

1 tbsp olive oil
1 brown onion, diced
1 clove garlic, minced
1 tsp cumin powder
1 tsp turmeric
1 tsp curry powder
8 chicken thighs
¾ cup coconut milk
¼ cup tomato ketchup
1½ cups chicken stock
2 tbsp peanut butter (health food shops often supply it fresh)
1 cup chopped green beans or peas
coriander to garnish

Every now and then I will introduce my kids to a new flavour—sometimes with disastrous results. I love to cook with herbs, but I've learned to add some of them after I have served up for the kids. This recipe was their introduction to curry. It's very mild. Remove the peanut butter if anyone in your family is nut intolerant.
— *Lisa*

1. Preheat the oven to 180°C.
2. Heat the olive oil in a pan and brown the onion and garlic, cooking for about 3 minutes.
3. Add the spices to the pan and stir through.
4. Add the chicken thighs and brown on each side.
5. Combine the coconut milk, tomato ketchup, chicken stock and peanut butter and add to the pan.
6. Pour the curry into an ovenproof dish and bake in the oven for 50 minutes, adding the greens to the dish after 25 minutes.
7. Garnish with coriander and serve with rice and some steamed carrots.

Serves 4

WHITE RICE
White rice is the most common rice. Available in long-, medium- and short-grain varieties, it is extremely versatile.

BROWN RICE
Brown rice is a less processed variety of rice. Also available in short-, medium- and long-grain, it is chewy and healthy with its layer of bran. Brown rice requires a longer cooking time than most other rice.

ARBORIO RICE
Arborio is a short-grain rice. It absorbs tastes when cooked and has a creaminess which comes from the starch released while cooking. Best cooked to an al dente stage, it is used for risottos and rice puddings.

SUSHI RICE
Sushi rice is a short-grain rice that sticks together and keeps its form when moulded, making it ideal for sushi.

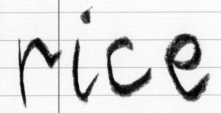

rice

Rice is consumed all around the world and the different varieties make it perfect for various applications. It can be used for any meal of the day. Rice is generally categorised by the size of its grain. The short-grain varieties are moist and stick together when cooked (good for puddings and risotto). Long-grain rice separates when cooked (good for main meals, paellas, etc.). — Lisa

BASMATI RICE

There are brown and white varieties of this long-grain rice. Used widely in Indian cooking, basmati is fragrant, with grains that separate when cooked.

JASMINE RICE

Jasmine is a fragrant long-grained rice favoured in Thai cooking. When cooked, its grains will be fluffy in texture.

WILD RICE

Wild rice is a form of grass found in swampy marshes. A native crop of North America, it is expensive due to the difficulties involved in its harvesting. Wild rice requires a longer cooking time, like brown rice, but has a wonderful nutty taste and is considered to be very healthy.

BLACK RICE

Black rice is cultivated in Asia and is a popular choice of rice for desserts. It is unmilled, making it high in fibre. Black rice has a long cooking time.

RICE COOKERS

Rice cookers are brilliant. Yes, it's easy to cook rice on the stove in a saucepan, but when you are busy with kids, a rice cooker is a great help. On some winter nights my kitchen bench has the rice cooker working away next to the slow cooker. I really try not to over-accessorize in the kitchen, but after sitting unused for two years in a cupboard, my rice cooker has reemerged! I usually cook enough for us to have daggy rice, milk and sugar for dessert - comfort food at its best.

Chicken & Bacon Towers

12 chicken thigh fillets
6 middle bacon rashers
2 tbsp olive oil
1 clove garlic, crushed
1 tsp Dijon mustard
3 tbsp parmesan cheese, finely
   grated
2 tsp thyme leaves
salt and pepper

toothpicks

Sometimes something as simple as food standing upright on the plate can be all it takes to lure a fussy eater to the table. The rest of them will come running for the can't-go-wrong combination of delicious flavours.
— *Di*

1. Preheat the oven to 180°C.
2. Trim the chicken fillets so that they are roughly rectangular in shape, and remove any fat or gristly bits. Trim the rind off the bacon and cut each length in half. Mix the remaining ingredients into a paste.
3. Lay down a strip of bacon, fat side on top, then place one of the chicken fillets over it (they should be roughly the same length). Smear a generous teaspoonful of paste along the chicken, mostly in the centre section.
4. Roll up the bacon and chicken together and secure the rolls with toothpicks.
5. Stand the rolled chicken towers upright in a greased baking dish (keeping the fat edge of the bacon at the top) and bake for approximately 40 minutes, or until cooked through.
6. Place the towers on plates and drizzle with the pan juices. One or two towers will serve a child, and cater for three per adult. Serve with a fresh garden salad.

Serves 4–5

LEFTOVER TOWERS

Try slicing leftover towers into tasty little discs for sandwich fillings. These swirls can also be a great ready-made pizza topping. Grab a pizza base or slice of pita bread, smear with tomato paste and decorate with sliced towers. Finish with a handful of mozzarella and bake at 200°C until the cheese melts and starts to brown.

Crumbed Lamb Cutlets with Mash & Honeyed Carrots

½ cup plain flour
1 cup breadcrumbs
½ cup parmesan cheese, grated
1 tsp thyme leaves
1 tbsp parsley, finely chopped
salt and pepper
lamb cutlets (approx. 12 for a family
  of 5)
2 eggs, lightly beaten with a dash of
  milk
3 tbsp olive oil
20 g butter

creamy mash
4 large potatoes, peeled and
  chopped evenly into large chunks
½ cup milk
25 g butter
salt and pepper to taste

honeyed carrots
1 bunch baby carrots (about 14)
2 tbsp honey
10 g butter

The lamb cutlet … dinner with a handle, dinner on a stick, dinner to eat standing up at a barbeque and, in my opinion, the sweetest cut of meat around, with a super high strike rate when it comes to feeding the family. All this makes the cost of these delectable little portions a worthwhile option every so often.
— *Di*

1. On a sheet of newspaper or greaseproof paper, make a pile with the flour on one side and then combine the breadcrumbs, parmesan, herbs and seasoning in a separate pile next to it.
2. Press the cutlets into the flour, flattening them slightly. Dip into the egg wash, then transfer them to the crumb mixture, coating the cutlets entirely.
3. Heat the olive oil and butter in a large pan and fry the crumbed cutlets until cooked through and browned on both sides.
4. Rest the meat on a paper towel for a couple of minutes before serving with the creamy mash and honeyed carrots (see below).

creamy mash
1. Boil the potatoes in a saucepan until cooked through (test the largest piece with a skewer). Drain well and return to the saucepan.
2. Add the milk, butter and seasoning and mash until well-combined and with a smooth texture. Add extra milk if the consistency is too thick.

honeyed carrots
1. Scrub the carrots and cook in boiling salted water for about 5 minutes. Drain and place in a bowl or serving dish.
2. Gently heat the honey and butter together in a saucepan and, when melted, drizzle over the carrots. Toss to coat.

Serves 5

The following are three handy variations.
These make terrific finger food at a barbeque
— *Lisa*

15 lamb cutlets
2 eggs, lightly beaten
2 cups grated parmesan cheese

Parmesan Crusted Cutlets

1. Dip individual cutlets in the beaten egg, then coat in the parmesan.
2. Place the cutlets on a baking tray and pop under a hot grill. Cook for 5–8 minutes on each side, depending on taste.

Makes 15 cutlets

15–20 lamb cutlets
juice of 2 lemons
½ tbsp flaked salt
2 tbsp dill, finely chopped

Lemon, Dill and Salt Cutlets

These are better if left to marinate for a few hours in the fridge prior to cooking.

1. On a large tray, lay out the lamb cutlets.
2. Mix together the lemon juice, salt and dill and pour over the cutlets. Turn them over to make sure they are well-covered and marinate for a few hours.
3. Barbeque or grill for 5–8 minutes on each side.

Makes 15–20 cutlets

½ cup redcurrant jelly
juice of 1 orange
1 tbsp orange zest
5 mint leaves, finely chopped
1 lamb rack

Tim's Rack

I found this handwritten recipe in my partner's pre-me cooking notebook.

1. Combine all the ingredients, except the rack of lamb, in a small saucepan over a medium heat and reduce the mix until caramelised.
2. Brush the syrup over the lamb rack and bake in the oven at 180°C for 40 minutes.
3. Serve with greens and buttered cocktail potatoes with continental parsley.

Serves 2

'All mothers are working mothers'
—Unknown

Spiky (Greek) Meatballs

meatballs
400 g mince lamb or beef
⅓ cup basmati rice
1 tbsp plain flour
1 small onion, grated
1 egg
25 g butter, melted and browned
2 tbsp water
1½ tbsp mint, finely chopped
salt and pepper

sauce
2 tbsp olive oil
1 garlic clove, crushed
1 small carrot, finely diced
1 celery stick, finely diced
700 g jar tomato passata
1½ tbsp tomato sauce
1 cup beef stock
¼ cup red wine

These rice-studded meatballs are a fun alternative to good old 'spag bol'. Using a similar set of ingredients, you can repackage the old favourite into an exciting new dinnertime winner.
— *Di*

1. Combine all the ingredients for the meatballs in a bowl. Shape with wet hands into ping-pong size balls.
2. Meanwhile, for the sauce, heat the oil in a large pan (one that has a lid), add the garlic and vegetables and cook until the vegetables have softened. Add the remaining ingredients and simmer for 5 minutes.
3. Drop the meatballs into the simmering sauce. They should sit almost fully covered in the sauce for about 40 minutes with the lid on. Turn the meatballs gently with a spoon once, halfway through the cooking process.
4. Serve on a bed of creamy mash (see recipe p. 110) or spiral noodles, sprinkled with parsley and/or grated cheese.

Serves 4–6

oils

Oils should be kept in a cool, dark place and sealed tightly. Exposure will cause it to go rancid. Some oils can carry the flavours of other foods, while other oils are specifically used for their taste, like hazelnut and almond oils.
— Lisa

VEGETABLE OIL
Vegetable oil is the most common of edible oils. Generally a blend of different oils, it has a very mild flavour and is good for baking.

OLIVE OIL
Olive oil is one of the most known and well-used oils in cooking. Extra virgin olive oil is considered the best. Olive oil is made from the pulp of the olive fruit and has a distinctive taste. It is the suggested oil for most of our recipes and is also great for use in salad dressings or sauces.

CANOLA OIL
Canola oil has a mild taste and works well for pan frying, deep frying and baking. It is a good source of omega 3 (found in fish) and it is rich in vitamin A.

SUNFLOWER OIL
Sunflower oil has a mild taste and is very versatile. It has a high smoking point, so can be used for frying, but also works as a base for dressings, sauces or mayonnaise. Use it as a substitute for vegetable oil in baking.

PEANUT OIL
Peanut oil doesn't transfer flavours. It has a bland flavour and is good for use at high temperatures.

SESAME OIL
Sesame oil is available in a light or dark variety. Light sesame is good for frying; dark sesame oil is used more for flavouring. This oil is mainly used in dressings for salads, or in Asian dishes, and should be used in small amounts.

GRAPESEED OIL
A light, aromatic oil, grapeseed oil provides a good base for infusions.

Sunday Leg Roast with Vegies & Greek-Style Beans

meat
1 leg of lamb
2 tbsp olive oil
salt and pepper
2 cloves garlic, sliced lengthways
½ cup water
rosemary sprigs

vegies
750 g potatoes, halved
  (6 medium-sized)
500 g carrots, halved lengthways
  (4 medium-sized)
500 g parsnips, (8 small-sized)
1¼ kg pumpkin, cut into wedges
500 g beetroots, quartered
  (4 medium-sized)
olive oil
salt and pepper
800 g fresh peas (preferably),
  shelled

Greek-style beans
400 g long green beans, trimmed
2 tbsp olive oil
1 small onion, diced
2 garlic cloves, finely chopped
1 × 500 g can crushed tomatoes
1 tsp sugar
salt and pepper

Gather round, pile up your plate, and share a meal, stories and maybe some wine. It's been another big week and everyone's busy as usual, so it's great to come together over a Sunday roast.
— *Di*

meat
1. Preheat the oven to 180°C.
2. Wash the lamb leg, then rub with the olive oil and seasoning. Pierce the meat with a sharp knife and stud with the garlic (to your taste).
3. Place the leg in a large baking dish and tip in the water. Add rosemary to the dish and stud some smaller sprigs into the leg. Roast in the oven for around 40 minutes per kilo of meat, plus an extra 20–30 minutes overall. (Remember to add the vegies to the dish approximately one hour before the end of cooking time.)
4. Test the meat with a skewer; if it's cooked the juices should run clear. When cooked, transfer the lamb to a wooden board and rest for 5–10 minutes before carving.

vegies
1. Chop the vegetables into large and roughly even-sized portions, leaving the skin on where possible. Coat all the vegies (except the peas) in the olive oil, then place some around the leg of lamb and put the remainder in a separate baking dish. Season, and roast for approximately one hour.
2. Boil the peas for 2 minutes, then drain and put into a serving dish with a knob of butter on top.

Greek-style beans
1. Parboil the beans, then dunk them in cold water.
2. Heat the oil in a saucepan, add the onion and garlic and braise before adding the tomatoes, sugar and seasoning. Simmer for 5 minutes, then add the beans and stir, covering them in the sauce. Cook for a further 3 minutes and transfer to a serving dish for the table.

Serves 6–8

Salts

Salt occurs naturally in almost all foods, but it's also a wonderful seasoning and if used properly will heighten the natural flavour of most foods. — Lisa

TABLE SALT
Table salt is the most common salt in domestic use. It has a fine texture, which makes it useful for measuring accurately. It is an all-purpose salt and is used from baking to the salt shaker. Iodised salt contains iodine. Originally added to salt for health purposes, it remains today.

MURRAY RIVER PINK SALT
This very delicate, naturally pink salt is Australian. It's my favourite. Use it in all applications.

SEA SALT
Sea salt is crystalline flakes of salt harvested from the sea. Just crush between your fingers and sprinkle.

ROCK SALT
Rock salt is chunky in appearance and takes much longer to dissolve if used for cooking. This is widely used in salt grinders.

KOSHER SALT
This all-purpose rough salt dissolves quickly and is popular in restaurant cooking.

Lamb Shank Casserole with Dumplings

lamb shanks

2 lamb shanks
¼ cup plain flour, seasoned
1 tbsp olive oil
1 stick celery, thinly sliced
1 leek, diced
1 clove garlic, crushed
1 can crushed tomatoes *or*
3 tomatoes, skinned, deseeded and
    chopped (see page p. 29).
1 tbsp Worcestershire sauce
3 cups beef stock

dumplings

2 cups self-raising flour
120 g cream cheese, chopped
½ cup milk
1 tbsp Dijon mustard
1 egg

Winter fare doesn't get any better than a recipe with lamb shanks. As it's a really popular cut during the cold months, it's a good idea to freeze a couple of shanks to have on standby. Cooked over a couple of hours, the meat is incredibly tender, so it's good for children that find meat difficult to eat because it's too chewy or gets stuck in their teeth. Serve the shanks with mash, or remove the meat from the bones and make these dumplings—they cook in the casserole and absorb the flavours.

— Lisa

1. Coat the shanks in the seasoned flour.
2. Using an ovenproof pan with a lid, sauté the celery, leek and crushed garlic in the olive oil.
3. Add the seasoned shanks to the pan and brown.
4. Once the lamb is brown, add the tomatoes, Worcestershire sauce and stock to the pan and bring to the boil. Reduce the heat, cover the pan and simmer for 1 hour 30 minutes.
5. Meanwhile, preheat the oven to 200°C.
6. To make the dumplings, sift the flour into a mixing bowl and rub the cream cheese into the flour.
7. In a separate bowl, use a fork to mix together the milk, mustard and egg.
8. Combine the egg mixture with the flour mixture until a dough forms. Roll the dough into small balls.
9. At the end of cooking time, remove the lamb meat from the shanks, discarding the shanks and returning the meat to the pan. Add the dumplings to the casserole and place in the oven for 30 minutes.
10. Serve with steamed beans and carrots, lightly salted.

Serves 4

Fish Fingers & Hand-Cut Chips

2 large pieces of flake
2 eggs, lightly beaten
2 cups breadcrumbs or hanayuki
  flakes (Japanese breadcrumbs)
potatoes, peeled
vegetable oil
sea salt

I do a fish meal for my kids once a week. This recipe is one way I can guarantee they will enjoy their seafood experience.

— *Lisa*

1. Cut the flake into finger-size pieces.
2. Dip the pieces of flake in the beaten egg and coat each piece in the bread-crumbs.
3. In a heavy-based pan over a medium heat, shallow fry the fish fingers in vegetable oil until golden.
4. For the chips, preheat the oven to 200°C.
5. Line a baking tray with baking paper.
6. Cut the potatoes into finger-length chip shapes. Toss them in vegetable oil and sea salt, place on the baking tray and cook in the oven for 40 minutes or until golden brown.

Serves 4 children

FLUFFY CHIPS
If you want fluffier chips, parboil the cut potatoes for
8 minutes. Allow to cool, then toss in a plastic bag
with ½ cup of plain flour and a pinch of sea salt.
Bake for 25 minutes in a moderate oven until golden.

'The day is finally here ... the table is set, decorations are hanging and everybody looks fabulous. It's going to be hard not to eat all that yummy food before our guests arrive!'

4

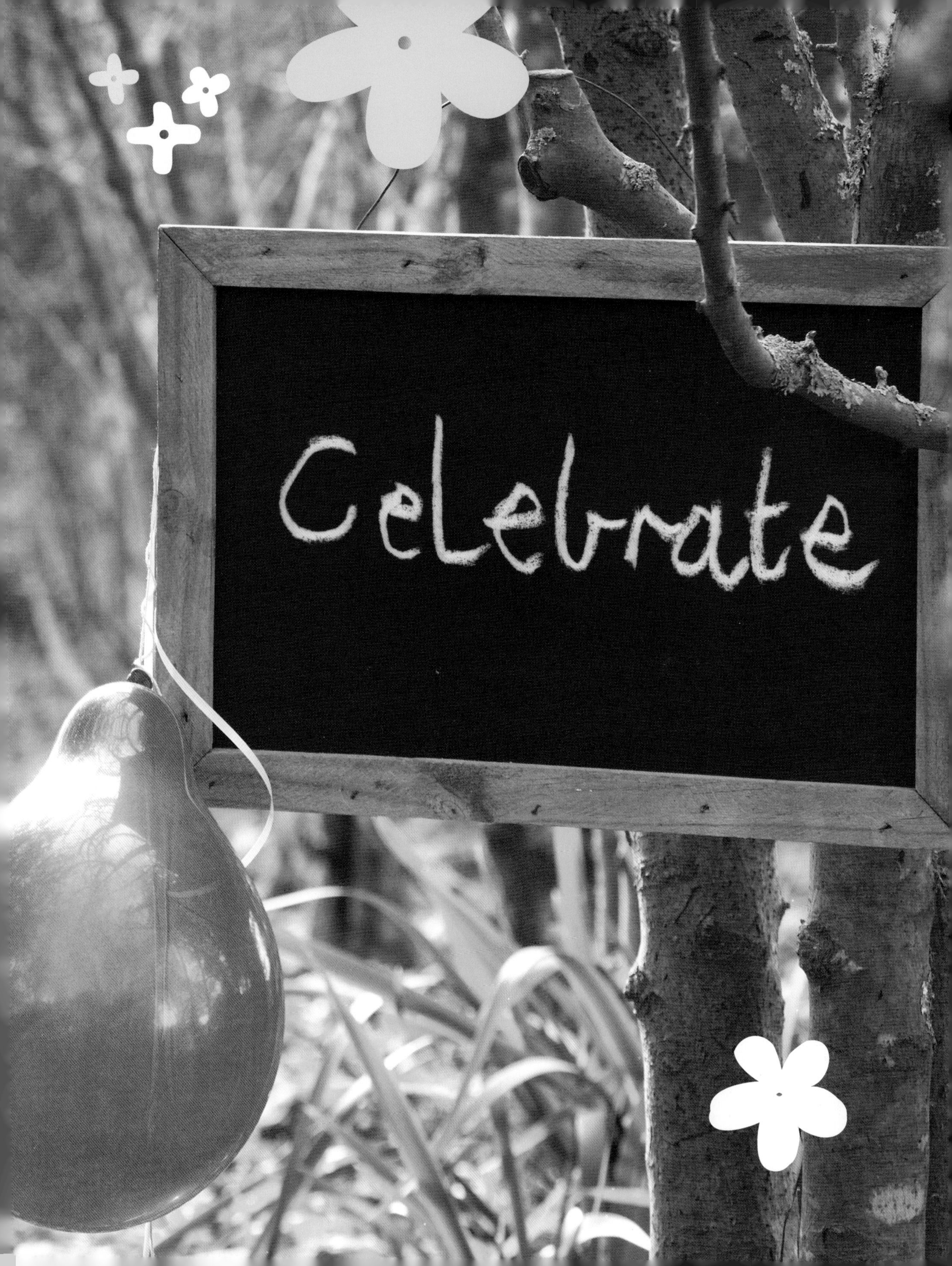
Celebrate

Fancy Pants Popcorn

¼ cup icing sugar
1 tsp cinnamon
½ tsp ground nutmeg
5 tbsp vegetable oil
½ cup popping corn
salt to taste

It's an oldie but a goodie. Dress it up for a party or serve it simply with a hint of butter and salt. This is a great party dish and post-celebration, it vacuums up in a flash.
— *Lisa*

1. Sift together the icing sugar, cinnamon and ground nutmeg.
2. You may wish to follow the instructions on the packet of popcorn you purchase. If not, place the vegetable oil in a large pot over a medium to high heat, adding a generous pinch of salt to the oil.
3. Place a few corn kernels in the pot and cover. When they spin or pop, add the remaining corn and cover with a lid.
4. Shaking regularly, continue to cook over the heat until all the corn has popped.
5. Transfer to a bowl or flutes and serve warm sprinkled with the icing sugar topping.

Serves 8+

ROLLED FLUTES
Paper flutes are very handy
for serving popcorn. To
make your own, take a
coloured square of paper
and roll it diagonally
into a cone shape.
Secure with tape and
voila, a rolled
flute for your
popcorn!

Ollie's Rocky Road

200 g quality milk chocolate
100 g dark chocolate
25 g butter
pinch of salt
¾ cup chopped marshmallows
1½ tbsp dried cranberries
1 tbsp desiccated coconut
⅓ cup crushed peanuts
⅓ cup macadamias, cut in half (if
   your kids don't like these, just
   leave them out)

My son Oliver asked for this to be named in his honour as he likes it the most. Here it is, Ollie! This rocky road makes a lovely gift in a large slab, or cut up in rocky pieces.
— Lisa

1. Melt the chocolate and butter, together with the salt, in a bowl over a pan of boiling water, stirring.
2. Once smooth, mix through all the other ingredients.
3. Place the mixture in a baking dish or tray (I use a ceramic 20 cm × 15 cm dish), then refrigerate for at least 3 hours.
4. Cut with a warm knife (it will make the cut smooth).

Makes 9 big pieces

SHAKE IT UP
Move things around a bit with
rocky road. My kids quite like it
with some chopped dried apricots
through the mix. If you have a nut
intolerance, or want to change the
'rocks', substitute the peanuts and
macadamias with Turkish delight or
glacé cherries chopped up. Pistachios
or broken biscuits would work well
instead of macadamias. Stop me now...

Patty Pan Toffees

3 cups caster sugar
1 cup water
¼ cup white vinegar
10 g butter
muffin-sized foil patty pans
sprinkles (hundreds and
   thousands)

Here's one version of the everlasting gobstopper!
– *Di*

1. Stir the sugar, water, vinegar and butter in a pan over a low heat until the
   sugar dissolves.
2. Increase the heat and bring the mixture to the boil, without stirring,
   for 10–15 minutes (or until the colour starts to change to a light golden
   brown). Pour directly into the foil patty pans, filling to about 1 cm deep,
   and sprinkle with hundreds and thousands. Leave to set.
3. For a softer, chewier toffee, cook for a shorter time (9–10 minutes).

Makes 15–20 toffees … perfect for the school fete!

party games

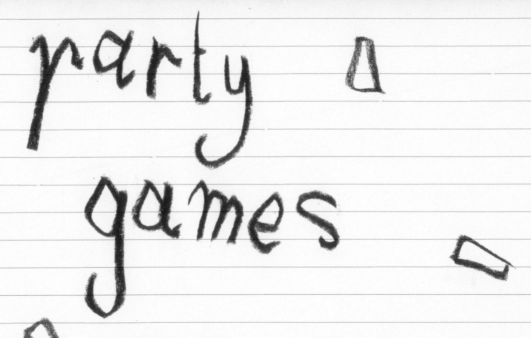

DANGLING DONUTS

This is an easy game to play at a kids' party.
Simply buy some donuts and suspend them from a line
with some string (1 donut per child). A Hills Hoist
in the backyard is brilliant for this. Players
cannot use their hands to eat the donuts and must
keep their hands behind their backs at all times.
Go!

THE CHOCOLATE GAME

For chocoholics, this one is a party favourite.
Put a block of chocolate on a plate with a knife
and fork in the centre of a circle of guests. Have
one die (or two if there are lots of people) that
everyone takes it in turns to roll. If someone rolls
a 6, then they hop into the circle and eat as much
chocolate as they can (with the knife and fork ...
tricky!) until someone else manages to roll a 6 and
takes their place. Continue until the block has been
demolished!

pto

EGG AND SPOON RACING

We all love the egg and spoon race. You may wish to set a course for the children to navigate or get them to simply run back and forth to each other over a 15-25 metre distance. All you need are some spoons and some eggs. You can use pre-boiled eggs or the more dangerous/fun uncooked egg. You could also elaborate on the idea, make teams and include a few extra legs in the race. Start with spoons and try something like marshmallows to ferry back and forth. The person has to then pass the marshmallow to the next member of the team, who has chopsticks, who in turn will transfer the marshmallow to someone with tongs. The first team across the finish line with the marshmallow wins!

WHAT'S THE TIME, MR WOLF?

Have an adult start as Mr Wolf, with their back turned to the children. All the kids stand a distance away and say in unison, 'What's the time, Mr Wolf?'

Mr Wolf then answers with a time, e.g. 'Its 5 o'clock'. The children must all then take 5 steps towards Mr Wolf.

(Mr Wolf is aiming to bring the children close enough to catch them, while the childrens' aim is to touch the wolf before he says, 'It's dinner time!')

The children keep asking, 'What's the time, Mr Wolf?' until he responds with 'It's dinner time!'

Mr Wolf then turns and chases the children, who are all running for the starting line. Whoever he catches becomes Mr Wolf.

DRESS-UP RACE
This game is a great icebreaker for large groups
when not everybody knows each other. You'll need a
big pile of clothes and dress-ups, including things
like shoes, hats, masks, ties, big tops, dresses,
beads, etc. Divide the guests into two teams. To
start the game, one person on each team has to run
over to the pile and choose one item to wear, get
into it and then run back to their team and tag
another member to go and do the same. Whichever
team is all dressed first wins!

TUG OF WAR
This game will bring out the competitive spirit in
everyone. Find a long piece of rope (the thicker the
better). Mark the centre and divide the party into
two even teams. Mark a centre line on the ground
and place the middle of the rope over this position.
Each team pulls their end of the rope until the
winning team forces their opponents over the centre
line. Victory!

THREE-LEGGED RACE
Pair up the children and tie the right leg of one
partner to the left leg of the other. In their
pairs they have to race the other teams to the
finish line. The first pair to cross the line are
the winners.

Marshmallows

vegetable oil
1 cup cold water
3 tbsp gelatin
¾ cup liquid glucose
2 cups caster sugar
¼ tsp salt
2 tsp vanilla essence
icing sugar for dusting

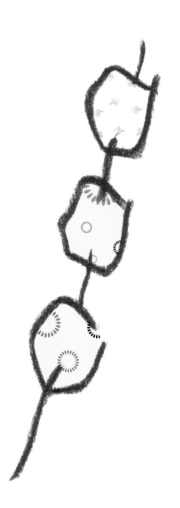

Marshmallows are a favourite, but overwhelmingly it is by the campfire that their legendary status is truly cemented. Speaking of cement, get a candy (or sugar) thermometer to make sure your marshmallow works; they're readily available and inexpensive (I picked one up for $6). I originally thought I could do it alone, but the thermometer made for an easy and successful cooking experience.
— *Lisa*

1. Line a large baking tray with baking paper and brush the paper with vegetable oil.
2. Put half of the water into the bowl of an electric mixer and sprinkle with the gelatin.
3. Place the liquid glucose, sugar, salt and remaining water in a heavy-based saucepan, and stir over a medium heat until the sugar has dissolved.
4. Once dissolved, increase the heat to boiling point, without stirring, using the candy thermometer to reach a temperature of 116°C (240°F), or 'soft ball' stage as it reads on the thermometer guide.
5. Once the mixture reaches the correct temperature, slowly pour it into the gelatin water in the electric mixer bowl, mixing as you do so on a slow speed.
6. When combined, increase the speed to high and mix for 12–15 minutes, adding the vanilla essence just before finishing.
7. Pour the marshmallow mixture into the lined baking tray. Place a second piece of baking paper over the top of the marshmallow and refrigerate overnight.
8. Using a large knife lightly greased with vegetable oil, cut the marsh-mallow into your desired shapes. I usually cut it into 2.5 cm cubes.
9. Dust or coat your marshmallow pieces with icing sugar.

Makes a large slab (36 cubes)

Marshmallow & Fruit Skewers

16 wooden skewers
1 rockmelon
½ watermelon
2 punnets strawberries
marshmallows

These colourful skewers are a healthy party option, and one that's always snapped up by frantic fingers—thanks, in part, to the cunningly placed marshmallows wedged in between the fruit.

— *Lisa*

1. Soak the skewers in water for half an hour before assembly.
2. Remove the skin and seeds from the rockmelon and cut into 2 cm cubes.
3. Repeat with the watermelon.
4. Remove the green stalks from the washed strawberries (if they are large strawberries, cut them in half).
5. Assemble the cut fruit and marshmallows onto the skewers.
6. With sharp scissors, cut the sharp points off the skewers.

Makes 16

Chocolate Spiders

2 tbsp peanut butter (crunchy if you prefer)
200 g milk cooking chocolate
1 packet Chang's Original Fried Noodles (gluten-free version available)
pinch of salt

The mere mention of these tasty little morsels is exciting to kids. When we talk about making them for a party, conversations start about collecting real spiders, roasting them in the oven to see if they would be crunchy, then substituting them at the party to see who would eat one. This recipe does contain nuts.
— Lisa

1. In a bowl, over a pan of boiling water, combine the peanut butter and chocolate until melted. Stir to achieve a smooth consistency.
2. Add the noodles and salt and coat them in chocolate.
3. Using a spoon, make small spiders with the mix and place them on a baking tray lined with greaseproof paper.
4. Refrigerate until set.

Makes 15–20 spiders

Coloured Jelly Orange Pieces

4 large oranges
2 packets different coloured jelly

This is a bright and appealing way to serve a small amount of jelly and is a perfect dish for 'take a plate' day at school.
— *Lisa*

1. Slice the oranges in half and gently remove the flesh and pith from each half. Be careful not to pierce the outer skin, or the jelly will leak through.
2. Place each orange half in a small ramekin bowl to give it support.
3. Make up the two jellies according to packet instructions and allow to cool.
4. Pour the cooled jelly into the orange halves and put them in the fridge to set.
5. Once the jelly is set, slice into the desired size. I make two pieces out of each orange half.

Makes approximately 16–24 jelly pieces

Tea Cup Marshmallows

1 packet Tic Toc biscuits
1 packet Freckles
1 packet white and pink
   marshmallows
1 packet Lifesavers
icing sugar mixed with a little water
   (for sticking)

These little marshmallow teacups are an easy hit for any kids' party. It's wonderful to watch their faces light up when they see something a bit different.
— *Lisa*

1. Use the biscuit as a saucer.
2. Use a little 'icing sugar glue' to secure the marshmallow to the biscuit. This is your cup.
3. Glue your freckle on top of the marshmallow (this is the froth), and add half a lifesaver for the handle.

Makes 20

```
BOTTLE IT
Why not make a collection of little
bottles for using at kids' parties?
Good food stores often sell six-
packs of juices. Simply drink the
juice and save the bottles. We
have a selection, which we put
strawberry and chocolate milkshakes
in. (You will need a funnel to help
pour the milkshake mix through the
tiny neck of the bottle.) It's a
little fiddly, but well worth the
effort. Simply add a straw!
```

LOLLY BAGS

Lolly bags are the traditional take-home treat at the end of a party. But they don't have to be full of lollies that will make your kids spiral out of control on a sugar high! In 2006, for my son's third birthday party, each of the kids took home a banana, a matchbox car, a few lollies and some stickers.

A banana in 2006 was significant as it was post Cyclone Larry and they were a luxury. Most of the kids peeled them and ate them walking out of the door. It was a parental epiphany. However, lolly bags are a great way to say thanks to your party guests, so spend a little creative time with the kids on them.
- Lisa

Chocolate Racers

Nestlé Melts, or icing sugar mixed
   with a little water (for sticking)
1 × 12-pack mini chocolate bars
1 pack Smarties
1 box Tiny Teddies

These are an absolute winner on the party circuit, and
so easy to assemble. I've used Mars bars or Milky Ways
in the past, but really you can use any mini chocolate
bar you (or the kids) like.
— *Lisa*

1. Either melt Nestlé Melts or combine icing sugar and a little water to
   create a 'glue'.
2. Stick your Smartie wheels onto the side of the chocolate bars. A Tiny
   Teddy can be poked into the chocolate bar as a driver, and add another
   Smartie for his steering wheel. Done.

Makes 12

party games

FREEZE DANCING/MUSICAL STATUES

All you need for this game is some space and a DJ on
the funky disco tunes, and soon the party will be
in full swing. The contestants must dance until the
music stops, then freeze. Those caught moving after
the music stops are OUT.

LUCKY PLATE PRIZE

Lucky Plate is a great way to entice the kids to the
table. When all the party guests are seated, have
them check under the plate in front of them (don't
forget to do this before serving the food!) for a
special marking (e.g. a smiley face drawn on the
plate, or a sticker). Whoever has the special symbol
is the winner of a prize!

'All that I am or ever hope to be, I owe to my angel mother.'
—Abraham Lincoln

Cup Cakes

125 g butter, softened
¾ cup caster sugar
1 tsp vanilla essence
2 large eggs, lightly beaten
2 cups self-raising flour, sifted
  3 times
pinch of salt
⅔ cup milk

butter cream (Vienna cream) icing
125 g butter, softened
1½ cups icing sugar
2 tbsp milk

I've made hundreds, perhaps thousands of cup cakes over the years, iced and decorated in a myriad of ways. I've used many different recipes, too, and while they are all fairly similar, I find Margaret Fulton's recipe from her *Encyclopedia of Food and Cookery* to be the lightest, fluffiest and most delicious of all. The extramoments spent re-sifting and adding ingredients at a gradual pace are well worth the effort!
— *Di*

1. Preheat the oven to 180°C.
2. Line cup cake tins with paper patty pans.
3. Cream the butter with an electric mixer. Add the sugar gradually and beat until smooth and creamy.
4. Gradually add the vanilla essence and the eggs, beating well after each addition.
5. Lightly fold through the sifted flour and salt alternately with the milk.
6. Spoon the cake mixture into the patty pan cases until they are three-quarters full. Bake in the preheated oven for 15 minutes, or until the tops are golden brown. Remove the patty pans from the tin and cool on a wire rack. Decorate with sifted icing sugar or an icing of your choice.
7. To make butter cream or vienna cream icing, beat the butter with an electric mixer until white. Gradually beat in half the icing sugar, then the milk, and finally the remaining sugar. Add food colouring if required. Add flavour if desired (e.g. essence, citrus zest or ⅓ cup sifted cocoa powder for a chocolate flavour).

Makes 24 cup cakes

The Train Cake

2 × 450 g pre-made sponge cakes
1 sponge roll

icing
250 g butter at room temperature
3 cups icing sugar
4 tbsp milk
4 different food colourings

decorations
Smarties
licorice (the type you can strip)
banana lollies
musk sticks
marshmallows
large Freckles or chocolate mint
  slice biscuits

This is special—definitely not unseen before, but guaranteed to put smiles on faces. I did back-to-back years of train cakes with my kids, who kept on asking for them. They love picking off the lollies from the different carriages, and I have a lot of fun putting it together. Having attempted Star Wars jet fighters (where the wafers caught on fire and had to be extinguished), this locomotive is a dream. My tip is to buy pre-made sponge cakes. My local bakery makes up large sponges, which I cut to make up carriages, or supermarkets also stock plain sponges.
— *Lisa*

1. Prepare a board for the cake. I use an off-cut I kept from the kitchen cabinetry and cover it in thick wrapping paper or foil. A hardware store will always help you out.

2. Cut your three train carriages to shape (approximately 12 cm × 8 cm). Cut your sponge roll to make the front engine.

3. To make the icing (this will cover and bind the cake together), beat the butter in an electric mixer until white. Gradually add the icing sugar and milk to the butter, alternating the two until the icing has a smooth and spreadable consistency.

4. You will need to divide the icing between four bowls to make four different colours. If you have a hand beater, use it to blend a couple of drops of food colouring in each bowl of icing.

5. Start with the icing for the front engine carriage as it's your largest surface area. Using a knife, cover your sponge roll in the chosen colour and form a small stack with off-cuts of sponge. Ice this in your chosen colour.

6. Repeat this process with the remaining carriages.

7. Now to decorate the carriages. Border each carriage top with a thin lico-rice strip. For the first carriage, add banana lollies, vertically arranged and gently pushed into the sponge top.

8. Vertically insert musk sticks into the icing of the second carriage, or cut down the carriage and store the musk sticks like logs piled high.

9. Finally, the marshmallow carriage.

10. You can add some plastic animals in the carriages—tall giraffes among the musk sticks, for instance, or a monkey poking his head out through the bananas.

11. Next, place 'wheels' on each carriage. Four Freckles or mint slices on each carriage look good. If using the mint slices, place a Smartie in the centre of each wheel, using leftover icing mix as your adhesive.

12. Use the remaining Smarties to enhance your engine and carriages.

13. Finally, create a track of licorice strips.

14. Refrigerate.

Mini Cheeseburgers

meat patties
500 g minced beef
1 small brown onion, grated
1 tbsp tomato ketchup
1 tbsp Worcestershire sauce
pinch salt
1 egg, lightly beaten with a fork

1 cup plain flour
olive oil
16 small dinner rolls
lettuce leaves, washed
tomato, thinly sliced
  cheese
wooden toothpicks

Little burgers are perfect for little fingers. Make the mince mix up the day before you need these to save time. Then, after they are made, just leave them warming until ready to serve.

– Lisa

1. Combine all the ingredients for the meat patties in a bowl.
2. Using a large tablespoon, scoop up a heaped amount of mixture and roll it into a small ball. Repeat until all of the mince has been used.
3. Roll each ball in the flour.
4. When ready to cook, spray olive oil into a non-stick frying pan and when placing each ball into the pan, flatten it off into a small patty shape.
5. Cook the patties on each side, then place in a warm oven until ready to serve.
6. Kids can assemble their own cheeseburgers, but at a party, or if they are busy, simply cut the rolls and layer with lettuce, tomato, a patty and cheese.
7. For decoration, and to hold the burger together, use flagged wooden toothpicks pushed through the middle of the burger.

Makes 16

Mini Sausage Rolls

500 g pork mince (you can use
  sausage meat or beef mince if
  preferred)
1 cup fresh breadcrumbs
1 egg
1 tsp tomato paste
1 tbsp parsley, chopped
salt and pepper
3 sheets frozen, ready-rolled puff
  pastry
1 egg, lightly beaten
tomato sauce to serve

It's party time, and amongst a smorgasbord of sweet
goodies it's nice to have a bit of something savoury to
nibble on.
— *Di*

1. Preheat the oven to 180°C.
2. Combine the mince, breadcrumbs, egg, tomato paste, parsley and
   seasoning in a bowl (using your hands usually works best!).
3. Cut each defrosted pastry sheet in half and place a row of the mixture
   along the centre of each sheet. Roll to enclose and cut to the desired size
   (I like them mini—around 4 cm).
4. Place seam down on a lined baking tray and brush with the lightly beaten
   egg. Bake in the preheated oven for about 30 minutes, or until golden
   brown.
5. Serve with plenty of tomato sauce.

Makes approximately 35

FREEZING FOR THE FUTURE
These sausage rolls freeze well and are a handy snack
to bring out when you're suddenly faced with a group
of hungry little (or big) tackers. Cover the rolls in
plastic wrap and freeze before cutting them to size.

It's Christmas morning. Santa's been and there are little piles of presents here and there, plus the odd bit of wrapping paper not yet scooped up. Everyone's dressed in something new and the orders start flying:

'Can you grab the good plates out of the cupboard?'
'Not those ones. Yeah, those ones.'
'Would somebody bring in the outdoor chairs? They'll need a wipe down.'
'Not that sponge, the one from the laundry.'

Bodies traverse the room this way and that, and our excitement heightens as the aroma of a Christmas feast wafts through the entire house. Everyone has a job; everyone a part to play. Men are sorting out ice and drinks, kids are busy tinkering with new toys, my brother's cracking jokes to loosen up my mother (it's her birthday on Christmas day), while my sisters and I make sure the table is set and the salads are made. It's my grandma's role to fry up the 'revithokeftedes'. Mum makes these little chickpea delights each Christmas and the fry-up ritual is not to be missed! The kitchen hits fever pitch as Mum and Yais (my grandma) begin to banter and argue:

'That's not enough salt!'
'Stop flipping them around, Mum!'
'Oh, you're beating the mixture!'
'The oil's too hot!'

As the fritters are lifted out of the oil, they get quickly swiped and eaten by passing traffic ... needless to say, there's a lot of hand slapping going on and it's usually just a small plate that makes it to the table! Christmas would certainly be a lot less colourful without them (the fritters and the frantic Greek ladies!).
- Di

Chickpea Fritters 'Revithokeftedes'

2 cups canned chickpeas, rinsed
and drained
1 cup water
1 onion
1 egg
1 slice white bread, crust removed
and torn
plenty of salt and pepper to taste
1 cup parsley, finely chopped
1 cup self-raising flour, or more if
required
olive oil for frying

1. Blend the drained chickpeas and the water in a food processor until they form a paste-like consistency.
2. Add the onion (chopped roughly), egg, bread and a generous amount of salt and pepper to taste. Blend together, then transfer to a bowl.
3. Mix in the parsley by hand (it's important not to add this into the blender as you'll end up with a green mixture), followed by the flour to thicken the mix. Add extra flour if the mixture is still too runny—it needs to hold together when frying.
4. Heat about 5 mm of olive oil in a large frying pan and drop in dessert-spoonfuls of chickpea mixture. Give them a little press with the back of a fork when they are frying so they end up as a flattish oval disc. Lower the heat and turn after about 2 minutes. When the fritters are golden brown on both sides, remove them and drain on layers of paper towel before serving.
5. Can be served warm or cold (if there are any left!).

Makes approximately 35

Chicken Nuggets

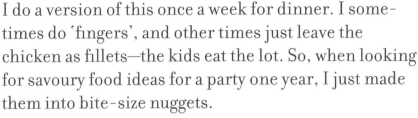

3 chicken breast fillets
1½ cups finely grated cheese
  (cheddar or parmesan)
2 cups breadcrumbs
2 eggs
60 g butter, melted

I do a version of this once a week for dinner. I sometimes do 'fingers', and other times just leave the
chicken as fillets—the kids eat the lot. So, when looking
for savoury food ideas for a party one year, I just made
them into bite-size nuggets.

— Lisa

1. Place the chicken, one breast at a time, in a press seal bag and use a ten-
   deriser or rolling pin to soften the breast.
2. Cut each breast into 4 cm squares.
3. Combine the grated cheese and breadcrumbs in a large bowl.
4. Whisk the eggs lightly in a separate bowl.
5. Line an oven tray with baking paper.
6. Coat the chicken squares in the egg, then roll them in the breadcrumb/
   cheese mix.
7. Using a pastry brush, coat the nuggets in the melted butter.
8. Place under a hot grill and cook for 5 minutes on each side.

Makes approximately 36

BREADCRUMBS ON HAND
Keep a stash of breadcrumbs in the freezer. You can
make your own with leftover bread, or buy bags of
them at the bakery. They always come in handy.

If you want to make your own breadcrumbs with those
unused end bits of the loaf, simply lay them out
on a baking tray, and dry them out in an oven set
at 150°C. Give them about 5 minutes on each side,
then remove and allow to cool. Place in a food
processor and reduce to the desired crumb texture.
It's particularly handy for those who are gluten
intolerant to have some breadcrumbs in the freezer.

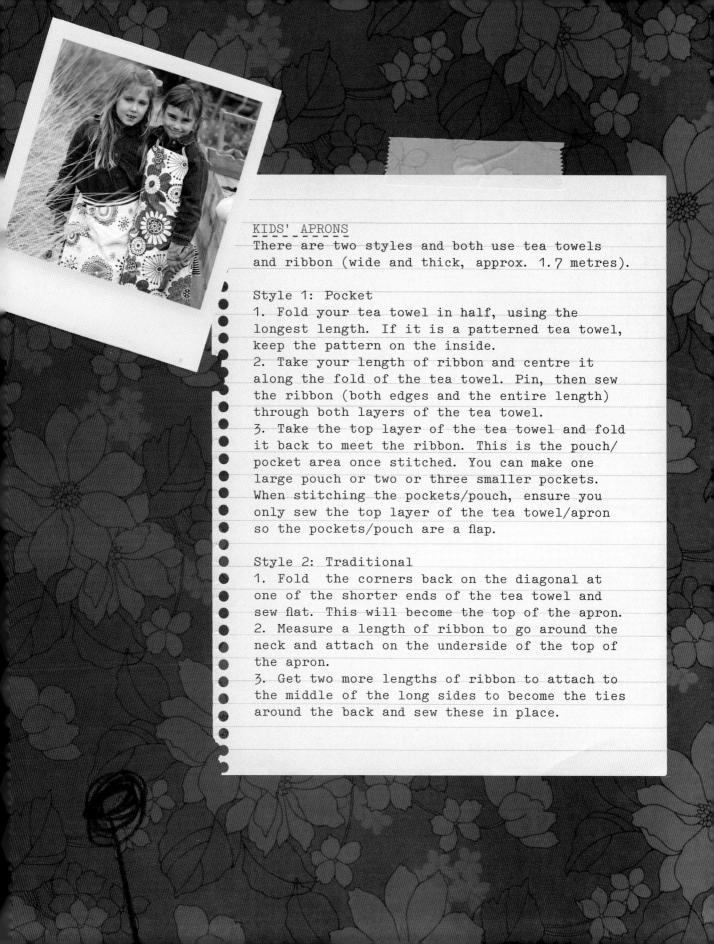

KIDS' APRONS
There are two styles and both use tea towels
and ribbon (wide and thick, approx. 1.7 metres).

Style 1: Pocket
1. Fold your tea towel in half, using the
longest length. If it is a patterned tea towel,
keep the pattern on the inside.
2. Take your length of ribbon and centre it
along the fold of the tea towel. Pin, then sew
the ribbon (both edges and the entire length)
through both layers of the tea towel.
3. Take the top layer of the tea towel and fold
it back to meet the ribbon. This is the pouch/
pocket area once stitched. You can make one
large pouch or two or three smaller pockets.
When stitching the pockets/pouch, ensure you
only sew the top layer of the tea towel/apron
so the pockets/pouch are a flap.

Style 2: Traditional
1. Fold the corners back on the diagonal at
one of the shorter ends of the tea towel and
sew flat. This will become the top of the apron.
2. Measure a length of ribbon to go around the
neck and attach on the underside of the top of
the apron.
3. Get two more lengths of ribbon to attach to
the middle of the long sides to become the ties
around the back and sew these in place.

5

Whether it's raining and pouring or the sunniest of days, I don't care; I'm always happy when I'm playing with you. Let's dress up, play our favourite game and laugh ourselves silly!

treasure hunt clues

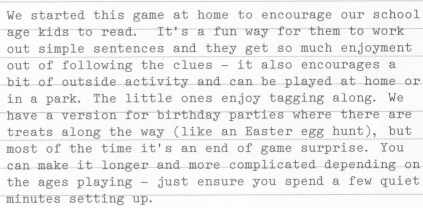

Clue #2

We started this game at home to encourage our school age kids to read. It's a fun way for them to work out simple sentences and they get so much enjoyment out of following the clues - it also encourages a bit of outside activity and can be played at home or in a park. The little ones enjoy tagging along. We have a version for birthday parties where there are treats along the way (like an Easter egg hunt), but most of the time it's an end of game surprise. You can make it longer and more complicated depending on the ages playing - just ensure you spend a few quiet minutes setting up.
- Lisa

RULES

1. Nobody can move off before the clue has been fully read.

2. It is a walking-only game. (Good luck.)

3. You have to do what's on the card and in the correct order (good for listening).

4. If there are treats, they must all be handed in at the end for even distribution amongst the players.

A 5-STEP EXAMPLE

An adult explains the game and the rules, then verbally gives the kids a hint as to where to find the first clue, e.g. 'You need to find the first written clue. In a room in the house is an instrument. It has keys. Here you will find what you need to continue. Go.'

Card 1 (sitting on the keys of the piano)
'Go out of the back door. Walk into the middle of the garden. Do three star-jumps. Look for the shoe to find clue 2. Go.'

Card 2 (in a shoe amongst other shoes scattered around)
'To find clue 3, find the tree that has a 3. Go.'

Card 3 (on the back of a cut-out number 3 hidden in a tree)
'You're getting better; now find a letter. Where might you choose to look?'

Card 4 (in the letterbox)
'Sing "Twinkle, twinkle little star" loudly with actions. Now walk inside and if you are able, under a table is your final clue. Go.'

Card 5 (stuck under a table)
'Time for afternoon tea! Well done!'

(When you are setting up the clues, write in the corner the location of where that clue should be placed; it stops you getting confused.)

'It is a happy talent to know how to play.'
—Ralph Waldo Emerson

CRAFT TABLE

Kids need a table that is a good working height for craft. It's also helpful if you can use a table outside for painting and messy play. An old, sturdy table, with the legs cut down to size is an easy, inexpensive way to accommodate those little legs.

playdough

Playdough is twice the fun when you and the kids make it yourself. Not only is it quick and easy to do, it'll last heaps longer than the pricey, store-bought options.
- Di

4 tbsp cream of tartar
2 tbsp cooking oil
1 cup salt
½ tsp food colouring
2 cups boiling water
2½ cups plain flour
glitter, sparkles, sequins or little beads (optional)

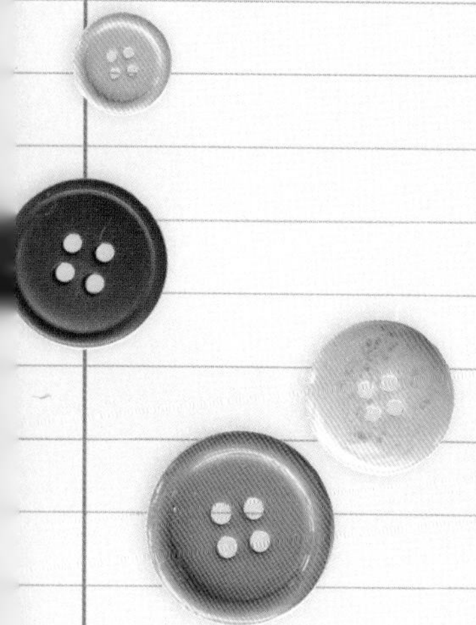

1. In a large bowl, combine the cream of tartar, oil, salt and food colouring with boiling water and whisk until most of the salt is dissolved. Allow to cool slightly.

2. Add the flour and mix until the liquid is absorbed.

3. Remove the dough from the bowl and knead on a bench top (sprinkle with a little extra flour if it's too sticky) until it holds together and becomes pliable.

4. For a bit of extra fun and 'bling', sprinkle some glitter or small decorations onto the playdough and knead them through.

Keeps for months in an airtight container.

shaving cream play

It's true to say that this activity can get a little
messy, but it's not as bad as it looks! If you keep
it outdoors and have a bucket of water (or a hose)
on hand, the kids can have fun cleaning up after
themselves. Ok kids, time to go wild!
- Di

1. If you are doing this on a window, spray the
   shaving cream onto the window and let the kids
   go for it - drawing, smearing, wiping and scraping.

2. If you don't have a suitable window, get a large
   tub or dish and let the kids play with the shaving
   cream in the tub - feeling the texture, making
   mountains, generally having a great tactile time
   with the shaving cream.

With both techniques, the possibilities and fun are
endless!

PUDDLING

This is what we self-titled our game of jumping in puddles. We parents spend so much of winter trying to keep the kids dry and warm. With this activity, however, they get wet and muddy. Slip on some gumboots and old gear, a beanie and a raincoat, and get out puddling. The more puddles the merrier. The kids get soaking wet, but the screams of riotous laughter are infectious. A warm post-puddling bath and a hot Milo is a pretty good combination, too.

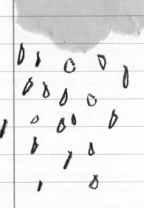

home made slime

Kids love the tactile experience of slime and this gooey recipe is basically just soap, so it's easy to deal with at pack-up time!
- Di

1 large plastic tub
1 box Lux soap flakes
warm water

1. Cover the base of your tub with soap flakes.
2. Pour in about 5 centimetres of warm water and mix with your hands, a whisk or a hand beater until the flakes have dissolved.
3. The slime will thicken as it cools – allow to cool completely before use.

flower power

Give some thirsty flowers a colourful drink and see
magic before your very eyes!
- Di

glass jars, cups or small vases
water
a range of different food colourings
fresh white flowers
scissors

1. Fill the glass vessels with water and add a few
   drops of food colouring into each.

2. Trim the flower stems and divide them between the
   glassware.

3. Leave the flowers in a warm room and watch them
   slowly change colour. The colours will intensify
   each day.

LIVING GIFTS
For housewarmings, Mother's
Day or birthdays, a potted
plant is a beautiful gift to
receive. The kids can help make
these ahead of time and might want
to paint the tubs. Plant some herbs
or flowers in small terracotta pots
and let them establish themselves for
a few weeks. Succulents are also good
for pots and don't require a huge
amount of watering.

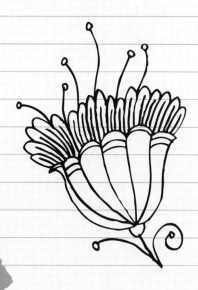

the garden

I have so many lasting sensory memories of times
spent exploring gardens as a child – the smell
of grass just after the rain, or jasmine on a warm
summer evening, finding crickets and frogs and
watching how they moved and where they were going.
A child can get lost inside their imagination for
hours in a garden. Remember what happened to Alice.

On weekends, when we might have some time to spend
in the garden, I enjoy listening to my kids. They
love to join in, digging in the earth for worms or
trying to catch butterflies. There are seldom any
flowers left after they have been pressed or used
for making up perfume potions. To them, the garden
is a wonderland.

You can get your kids involved in little garden
projects. It's quite easy to find child-size
gardening tools, some gloves and a mini watering
can. Depending on the size of your backyard, a
vegie patch can provide them with hours of fun,
and you with a few basics. In summer, some different
varieties of lettuce and tomatoes are salad
essentials you will use every day. Plant a lemon
tree (particularly handy for toilet training boys),
and in a few years you will benefit from its fruit.
A collection of usable herbs for cooking is a good
idea. I like having some herbs in pots so I can move
them around and occasionally bring them inside.
Pots are good if you live in an apartment or unit.
Do some research into your garden soil, position
and the suitability of the plants you intend to use
before you start.
- Lisa

teddy bear's picnic

The humble teddy bear biscuit is the perfect
vehicle for some decorative fun and games. Throw
a blanket across the lawn, pack the picnic basket
full of treats and prepare for an afternoon of
sweet creativity and yummy fun!
- Di

1 packet plain teddy bear biscuits
licorice allsorts
M&M Minis
1 or more quantities/colours icing
greaseproof paper rolled into piping bags
sticky tape

ICING
½ tbsp margarine
1 ½ tbsp boiling water
1 cup icing sugar
2 drops food colouring

1. Make the icing by putting the margarine into a
   bowl and adding the boiling water and sugar, then
   the food colouring. Mix with a bread and butter
   knife or metal spatula until the margarine has
   melted and the colour is even.

2. Make small piping bags by rolling a piece of
   baking paper into a cone, securing with sticky tape
   and then snipping a small opening at the pointy end.

3. Pull apart the licorice allsort layers, and using
   a small, sharp knife, cut shapes for the teddies
   to wear, e.g. bow ties, mittens, buttons and belts.

4. Fill the piping bags with spoonfuls of icing and
   use to pipe decorations onto the biscuits. Dobs
   of icing can also be used to adhere the licorice
   shapes and M&Ms to the biscuits.

potato printing

Forget about impersonal and expensive store-bought wrapping paper and cards. Grab some old spuds and set up your own potato printing production line!
- Di

medium to large potatoes
acrylic paint
paintbrush
paper or card

1. Cut the potatoes in half.
2. Choose a simple shape, letter or image and mark it onto the cut side of the potato.
3. With a sharp paring knife, carefully cut away the negative area of your chosen shape 5-10 millimetres deep.
4. Paint the image generously, then stamp it onto card or paper. Paint will need to be reapplied after every 3 or 4 stampings.
5. Leave the paper to dry. Further decorate your stamped paper and cards with pens, pencils or glitter if desired.

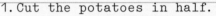

wrapping paper art

When kids start at kindergarten, there is an endless supply of amazing artworks that come home. My very creative husband started using these masterpieces as wrapping paper for gifts. It's a lovely personal touch and it makes the emerging young artists very proud.

card making

Receiving a handmade gift or card is really special. Di makes beautifully illustrated cards that have become keepsakes in our children's collections. I possess little illustrative ability, but I do a particularly good decorated swing tag. Having time is always the difficulty, but if you have the 'what you need' items at hand, it's more achievable. Grab some boxes and fill them with decorating items—ribbon, string, stickers, or whatever else you may discover in your travels. A good glue, scissors, a ruler, a cutting mat and a Stanley knife will come in handy. If you have access to the Internet, there are some great websites you can look at for ideas. The kids will enjoy you sitting down with them to do this activity.

op shopping

At the local op shop you will find great items to entertain the kids. From dress-ups to toys and books, the list of items to be reused and recycled is endless. It's an inexpensive way to let your kids use their imaginations.

Recently, the kids had a dress-up day at school. One wanted to go as Indiana Jones, the other as Jack Sparrow. We found so many great accessories for their outfits down at our local op shop. Why not make a donation and recycle at the same time?

dress-ups

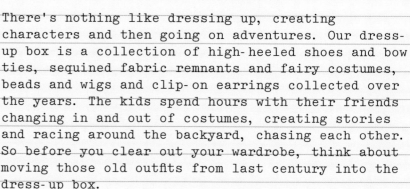

There's nothing like dressing up, creating characters and then going on adventures. Our dress-up box is a collection of high-heeled shoes and bow ties, sequined fabric remnants and fairy costumes, beads and wigs and clip-on earrings collected over the years. The kids spend hours with their friends changing in and out of costumes, creating stories and racing around the backyard, chasing each other. So before you clear out your wardrobe, think about moving those old outfits from last century into the dress-up box.

'Do not go where the path may lead; go instead where there is no path and leave a trail.'
—Ralph Waldo Emerson

'It's just you and me. Let's relax, hang out and spoil ourselves. We can discuss all our favourite things in life and share our sweet secrets!'

6

Nic's Biscuits

This treat had to be included at the insistence of my son, Archer. Our very wonderful neighbour made these after school one day and he never stops talking about them. The ginger biscuit base could be substituted with homemade ginger biscuits if you get the time.
— *Lisa*

cream cheese at room temperature
  (there is a spreadable version
  available)
strawberries

gingernut biscuits
1. Take a single biscuit and, using a knife, spread a thick layer of cream cheese on top.
2. Decorate with sliced strawberry. (You can slice vertically into the strawberry and then fan it out for a more decorative look.)
3. That's it! Serve with a glass of cold milk or a smoothie.

2 cups plain flour
¾ cup caster sugar
½ tsp bicarbonate of soda
1 tsp cinnamon
1 tsp ground ginger
pinch salt
pinch ground cloves (optional)
125 g butter (at room temperature)
1 egg
1 tbsp golden syrup
1 tsp black treacle

homemade ginger biscuits
1. Preheat the oven to 180°C.
2. Sift together all the dry ingredients into a mixing bowl.
3. Rub the butter into the dry mixture.
4. In a separate bowl, beat the egg, syrup and treacle together, then add to the biscuit mixture.
5. Using your hands, work the mixture into a dough, then make small balls from the dough.
6. Place each ball on a baking tray lined with baking paper (about an inch apart) and bake for 10–15 minutes.
7. Remove the biscuits from the oven and leave to cool on the baking tray—the biscuits will firm up as they cool.

Makes 15–18 biscuits

Chewy Brown Sugar Pavs

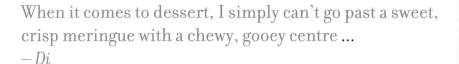

4 egg whites
½ cup caster sugar
½ cup brown sugar, firmly packed
1 tsp lemon juice
1 tbsp cornflour
1½ cups thickened cream
fresh fruit such as mango,
   passionfruit or berries

When it comes to dessert, I simply can't go past a sweet, crisp meringue with a chewy, gooey centre ...
— Di

1. Preheat the oven to 120°C.
2. Whisk the egg whites on high speed in the large bowl of an electric mixer until soft peaks form.
3. Lower the mixer speed and gradually add the combined sugars, one tablespoon at a time.
4. When firm peaks have formed and the mixture has a satiny sheen, add the lemon juice and cornflour. Fold in by hand until combined.
5. Place large spoonfuls of the meringue onto lined baking trays and form into 8 cm rounds with some space in between.
6. Bake in the oven for 50 minutes. After this time, turn the oven off and allow the meringues to cool while inside.
7. Serve topped with whipped cream and fresh fruit of your choice.

Makes 8–10 pavs

MINI MERINGUES
Sometimes I use this recipe to make trays of bite-size
meringues. Fabulous for parties, I'll often add some sprinkles
or cachous for a touch of sparkle and fun. Tablespoon-sized dobs
of mixture take only around 25 minutes to cook. Just add your
sprinkles before they go into the oven.

'All the world is made of faith, and trust, and pixie dust.'
—J. M. Barrie

Andy's Caramel Cups

1 packet butternut snap biscuits
1 × 380 g can Nestlé Top'n'Fill Caramel
1 cup whipped cream
10 g piece milk chocolate, finely grated or
2 tbsp sprinkles

I was served this wonderfully simple and speedy to assemble dessert after a dinner at my friend Andy's house about ten years ago. They're so cute and scrumptious that it's almost impossible to eat just one, but beware, they're rather rich!
— Di

1. Preheat the oven to 150°C.
2. Place the biscuits over the holes of a cupcake tray, then place the tray in the preheated oven for 7 minutes to soften the biscuits.
3. Remove the tray from the oven and gently push down the centre of each biscuit to form a little bowl shape. Leave to cool and reharden.
4. Fill each cup-shaped biscuit with a teaspoon of caramel, then top with a dollop of whipped cream and either chocolate shavings or sprinkles.

Makes 21 cups

Honeycomb

4 tbsp golden syrup
1 cup caster sugar
3 tsp bicarbonate of soda
½ cup milk or dark chocolate buttons or buds, melted

Crunchy and melt-in-your-mouth, these sweet little chunks of honeycomb are a great indulgence to have at home, or to package up for the movies or your next road trip.
— Di

1. Mix together the golden syrup and sugar in a large saucepan and simmer over a low heat for approximately 7 minutes.
2. Remove from the heat and add the bicarbonate of soda, stirring quickly through. Pour into a lined slice tin to set (the mixture begins to set very quickly, so you must work fast!)
3. Drizzle the melted chocolate over the set honeycomb. (Melt more buds if it's a solid layer of chocolate you desire.)
4. When the chocolate has hardened, remove the honeycomb from the tin and break into rough chunks, or cut with a serrated knife. Any leftover shards make a delicious ice-cream topping.

Makes 40–50 pieces

HONEYCOMB GIFTS
Grab a handful of clear cellophane bags and some thin ribbon or string, then bag up some lovely homemade gifts. Bags of honeycomb are a quick and economical cake stall or school fete winner.

Sesame Caramels

½ cup sesame seeds, toasted
90 g butter
2 tbsp honey
1 cup brown sugar
⅓ cup liquid glucose
½ cup condensed milk
¼ cup sunflower seeds

I'm yet to completely sell sesame seeds to the entire family, but I'm working on it. These bite-size caramels make a great gift in a decorated jar—just try not to eat them all before you give some away.
– Lisa

1. Line a baking tray with baking paper and lightly toast the sesame seeds under a hot grill for 3–5 minutes, giving them a shake halfway through. Set aside.
2. Combine the butter, honey, brown sugar, glucose and condensed milk in a heavy-based pan over a medium heat.
3. When the sugar has dissolved, bring the caramel mix to the boil, stirring. Use a candy thermometer and continue to boil until the caramel reaches 'firm ball' stage (120°C).
4. Add the sunflower seeds and half of the toasted sesame seeds to the caramel.
5. Pour into a lined 29 × 19 cm baking tray and allow to cool.
6. Once cooled, cut into approximately four long strips of caramel. Fold each length in half, and roll into a log shape. Coat the caramel pieces in the remaining sesame seeds and refrigerate for at least 2 hours. Cut into round pieces when chilled.

Makes approximately 40 pieces

Sugars

Most of us consume some form of sugar every day. Here are some of the most common — Lisa

UNREFINED RAW SUGAR
Unrefined raw sugar is made from the juice of the sugar cane. Used in cooking and baking, it has a crunchy consistency.

CASTER SUGAR
Caster sugar is a fine sugar that dissolves easily. It is used for making biscuits, cakes and pastries.

BROWN SUGAR
Brown sugar is a dark, moist sugar. This moisture is good for cake and biscuit making and for butterscotch. Lighter brown sugars are used for condiments and sauces. Demerara (large brown crystals) and muscovado (very dark brown) are other varieties of brown sugar.

ICING SUGAR
Icing sugar is a crushed form of sugar, used mostly for icings. Pure Icing Sugar is, as it says, pure. You can also buy Icing Sugar Mixture, which has a small amount of cornflour added. Pure Icing Sugar is the one to use if you're gluten intolerant.

PALM SUGAR
Palm sugar is a sugar from a type of palm tree.
Used mostly for Thai or Asian dishes, it provides
a balance between dishes that use hot, sour or
salty ingredients. You will often find it grated
or chopped.

MOLASSES, OR TREACLE
Molasses is commonly used for gingerbread and
licorice. It is not necessarily used for sweetness,
but for darkness of colour, and is often used in
conjunction with other sugars.

GOLDEN SYRUP
Golden syrup is a pale treacle used in a lot of
biscuit making, sometimes as a substitute for honey
or as an alternative to corn syrup.

MAPLE SYRUP
Maple syrup comes from the sap of the maple
tree. Its expense is due to the refining process and
its short harvesting time of six weeks. Maple syrup
is great for use as a topping, or for glazes.

GLUCOSE SYRUP
Glucose syrup is derived from corn. It is used in
toffees, caramels and other candies as the melting
point starts at a lower temperature and therefore
caramelises quicker.

Passionfruit Slice

base
1 cup self-raising flour
1 cup desiccated coconut
125 g butter, melted
½ cup caster sugar

top
1 × 395 g can sweetened condensed
  milk
½ cup lemon juice
5 tbsp passionfruit pulp (3 or 4
  passionfruits should do)

There are no nuts, eggs or seeds in this sweet treat,
making it safe to bring out anytime, anywhere—a good
one to whip up for the school or kinder cake stall.
— *Di*

1. Preheat the oven to 165°C.
2. Combine the base ingredients in a bowl, then press firmly into a lined
   baking tin of approximately 17 cm × 25 cm × 4 cm. Use the bottom of a
   glass to help compact the biscuit base.
3. Bake the base in the oven for 15 minutes.
4. Meanwhile, combine the ingredients for the topping in a bowl.
5. Remove the base from the oven and cool for 5 minutes before pouring
   the passionfruit mixture over the top. Return to the oven and bake for a
   further 15 minutes.
6. Use the sides of the baking paper to help you lift the slice from the tin,
   then cool on a wire rack before cutting into portions.

Makes approximately 16 pieces

Corey's Brownies

200 g margarine
2 cups caster sugar
4 eggs
1½ tsp vanilla essence
⅔ cup plain flour
⅔ cup cocoa powder
1 cup dark chocolate buttons or
  buds
1⅓ cups walnuts, roughly crushed
2 tbsp vegetable oil

Sometimes we all crave a bit of chocolate in our lives and this brownie is sure to satisfy. Since Corey handed me his special recipe, I've been making it on repeat at home, and although his secret ingredient—a last minute splash of vegetable oil—is designed to make these brownies last longer, I've found that to be a little unnecessary!
— *Di*

1. Preheat the oven to 180°C.
2. Cream the margarine and sugar together in an electric mixer. Add the eggs and vanilla essence and mix to combine.
3. Sift the flour and cocoa powder and add to the mixture. Mix on low speed to combine.
4. Fold through the chocolate buds and walnuts, followed by the vegetable oil.
5. Put the brownie mixture into a lined baking tray approximately 23 cm × 23 cm × 6 cm.
6. Bake in the oven for about 45 minutes. (It should be crisp on top and still moist in the centre.)
7. Dust with extra cocoa or icing sugar and serve with vanilla ice-cream and/or double cream for the ultimate indulgence! Keeps up to 10 days in an airtight container.

Serves 16

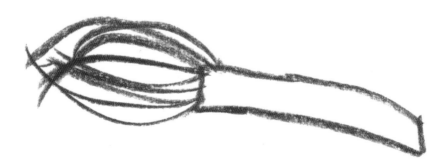

'Plunge boldly into the thick
of life, and seize it where you
will, it is always interesting.'
—Johann Wolfgang von Goethe

Chocolate Ripple Log

300 ml thickened cream
1 tbsp caster sugar
1 tbsp vanilla essence
1 packet chocolate ripple biscuits
chocolate Flake, Peppermint Crisp,
  or other decoration

When I was growing up, barely a dinner party went by without a chocolate ripple log. I remember waking up in the morning and raiding the fridge for leftover desserts. Of course, Mum's biscuits had been soaked in marsala, which I am not opposed to, but if making it for the kids you may prefer the non-dipsomaniac option. This ripple log is very easy to make and assemble—it just requires a little fridge time.

— Lisa

1. In a mixer, combine the cream, caster sugar and vanilla essence. Beat until the cream has thickened (approximately 7 minutes).
2. To create your log, place a dollop of the cream between two biscuits to bind them. Continue with this method, adding one biscuit at a time.
3. Cover the log with the remaining cream.
4. My Mum sprinkled a Flake on top, but choose your favourite decoration.
5. Refrigerate for about 6 hours or overnight.

Serves 8
Double the quantities if you wish your log

Pineapple Upside-Down Cake

50 g butter, melted
½ cup brown sugar
1 × 440 g can pineapple slices in
  juice, drained (keep the juice)
100 g butter, softened
½ cup caster sugar
1 egg
1 tsp vanilla essence
1¼ cups self-raising flour
½ tsp salt
½ cup pineapple juice

An oldie but a goodie!
— *Di*

1. Preheat the oven to 180°C.
2. Line the sides of a 20 cm round (or ring) non-stick cake tin with baking paper. Pour the melted butter into the tin and sprinkle with the brown sugar. Arrange the pineapple slices on top.
3. Cream the softened butter and caster sugar together in an electric mixer. Add the egg and vanilla essence and continue beating until fluffy.
4. Sift the flour and add to the mixture with the salt. Slowly incorporate the retained pineapple juice.
5. Pour the cake batter into the tin, over the pineapple layer. Bake in the oven for about 45 minutes. You can test the cake to see if it's ready by inserting a skewer into the centre of the cake. If the skewer comes out clean, the cake is ready.
6. Serve warm or at room temperature, with cream.

Serves 8–10

Kids' Individual Apple Tarts

2 sheets puff pastry
1 tsp ground cinnamon
2 tbsp caster sugar
2 egg whites, whisked
3 large apples, cored and quartered
  then thinly sliced
2 tbsp jam

With pastry from the freezer, apples from the fruit bowl, sugar from the pantry and a little jam of any flavour, these individual servings make a perfect (and perfectly easy) little dessert, or pastry addition to a morning tea with friends.

— *Lisa*

1. Preheat the oven to 200°C.
2. Cut each pastry sheet into four equal parts. This will make eight squares.
3. Lightly score the pastry sheet a couple of centimetres in from the edge.
4. In a bowl, mix together the cinnamon and sugar.
5. Brush the pastry with the whisked egg whites, then sprinkle with the cinnamon and sugar mix.
6. Lay the apple slices, overlapping slightly, within the scored square on each pastry piece.
7. Bake for 20–25 minutes, or until golden.
8. Mix a little boiling water with the jam and brush over the baked tarts.

Makes 8 pastries

Mango Mousse

1 × 425 g can mangoes or 2 fresh
  mangoes
1 cake of tofu from a 375 g pack,
  rinsed and drained
2 tbsp caster sugar
mint leaves to decorate

Mangoes are one of our most versatile fruits. At
Christmas time, when they are most bountiful, I buy
trays of them at the markets and use them in salads,
in milkshakes, or for a simple dessert. This mousse
uses silken tofu. Not everyone loves the texture of tofu,
but this is worth a try.
— *Lisa*

1. Put the mangoes, tofu and sugar in a blender and puree until smooth.
2. Pour into serving glasses and refrigerate for 30 minutes, or until set.
3. Garnish with the mint leaves and serve.

Serves 4

Chocolate Mousse

200 g block good quality chocolate
(I use 70% cocoa for adults, or
milk chocolate for the kids)
1 egg, whisked
200 ml cream

This recipe was passed on to me from a neighbour. She is a wonderful cook and entertainer, and is now living back in Germany with her Australian husband and little girl. She made this simple mousse one evening, and I absolutely loved it. It is very rich, so serve it in small quantities, perhaps with a little fruit. She maintained good quality chocolate was essential for making a good chocolate mousse. Enjoy. (Then go for a brisk walk.)
— Lisa

1. Place the chocolate in a mixing bowl over steaming water and stir until melted.
2. When melted, allow the chocolate to cool, then whisk the egg into the chocolate mix. Place in the fridge to chill.
3. Whip the cream in a separate bowl.
4. Carefully combine the whipped cream with the chilled chocolate. Refrigerate the mousse for 2 hours.
5. Serve a small amount with fruit.

Serves 4

'When the first baby laughed for the first time, the laugh broke into a thousand pieces and they all went skipping about, and that was the beginning of fairies.'
—from 'Peter Pan' by J. M. Barrie

Classic Sticky Date Pudding

date pudding

250 g dates, stoned
1 cup water
1 tsp bicarbonate of soda
60 g butter, softened
¾ cup caster sugar
2 eggs
¼ tsp vanilla essence
1¼ cups self-raising flour, sifted

caramel sauce

1¼ cups thickened cream
1 cup brown sugar
30 g butter
½ tsp vanilla essence

Be sure to save enough room for this crowd-pleasing dessert!
— Di

1. Preheat the oven to 180°C.
2. Place the dates, water and bicarbonate of soda in a small saucepan over a medium heat. Stir, and cook until the mixture goes jam-like and the dates are softened.
3. Cream the butter and sugar together in an electric mixer until pale and creamy. Add the eggs one at a time, beating well after each addition. Add the vanilla essence and then fold in the sifted flour.
4. Finally, stir in the date mixture until well-combined. Pour the mixture into a lined 20 cm × 20 cm cake tin and bake for around one hour (or until an inserted skewer comes out clean).
5. To prepare the caramel sauce, combine all the ingredients in a small saucepan and bring to the boil, stirring to dissolve the sugar. Continue to boil for 5 minutes to thicken.
6. Cut the warm date cake into portions, pour over the caramel sauce and serve with vanilla ice-cream if desired.

Serves 8—10

Creamy Rice Pudding

3 cups milk
1 cup thickened cream
1 vanilla pod
3 tbsp caster sugar
¼ tsp ground cinnamon
pinch grated nutmeg
1 tbsp grated orange zest
½ cup arborio rice
orange juice on hand for extra
 liquid if required
½ cup sultanas

Rice pudding is comfort food at its best—old-fashioned, but ever so satisfying. This version uses arborio rice; it makes for a chewier rice pudding. I have had this hand-written recipe stapled into the back of my collection book for a decade, and it has been well-used! You need to be a little more attentive with this stove recipe than with an oven version, but it's worth it.
— *Lisa*

1. In a heavy-based saucepan, over a medium heat, combine the milk, cream and vanilla pod. Once the milk starts to bubble, remove the pan from the heat.
2. Combine the sugar, cinnamon, nutmeg and orange zest, then stir into the milk and cream liquid.
3. Place the saucepan back over a medium heat and add the arborio rice.
4. Continue to stir for approximately 20 minutes. If you need more liquid in this time, add some fresh orange juice—no more than ⅓ cup at a time. Halfway through the cooking time, add the sultanas.
5. When the rice is cooked (almost tender), turn off the heat and allow to stand for 5 minutes.
6. Remove the vanilla pod from the rice pudding and serve, hot or cold.

Serves 6

Dollops of jam are always nice in plain rice puddings. —Lisa

Orange Parfait

4 egg yolks
½ cup orange juice
1 tbsp orange zest (optional)
2 cups whipping cream
½ cup caster sugar

I discovered parfaits a few years ago at Christmas time, when I was making a pavlova and had leftover egg yolks. (To be honest, quite a few things with the pavlova didn't go to plan.) However, all was well by the time Santa and the Christmas guests arrived. Lunch went smoothly, followed by a sensational pavlova topped with fig, raspberry coulis, passionfruit AND an orange parfait on the side. Small pat on the back to self.
– Lisa

1. Line a rectangular (23 cm × 14 cm × 6 cm) loaf tin with baking paper.
2. In a bowl, over boiling water, whisk together the egg yolks, orange juice and zest. Allow to cool.
3. Meanwhile, whip the cream in an electric mixer, gradually adding the sugar, until firm.
4. Fold the cooled orange mix into the cream and pour into the prepared tin.
5. Place in the freezer overnight, or for at least 6–8 hours. Serve with berries or fruit.

Serves 8

Summer Fruits & Macaroons with Vanilla Yoghurt

3 white peaches
3 white nectarines
6 apricots
¼ rockmelon cut into 1 cm cubes
1 cup cherries
1 cup grapes
1 cup berries
1 tsp lemon juice
1 passionfruit

macaroons
½ cup sugar
2 cups desiccated coconut
2 egg whites

Summer fruits are completely enticing. Complemented with some easy-to-make mini macaroons, this fruit salad is a delight to the senses. We recommend you go back for seconds. The fruit combinations below are suggestions—change the types and quantities of fruit according to tastes.

— *Lisa*

1. Rinse all fruit and de-seed the stone fruit.
2. Cut the peaches, nectarines and apricots in half, then each half into two pieces lengthways.
3. Discard the skin from the rockmelon and cut the flesh into 1cm cubes.
4. Place the cut stone fruits, rockmelon, cherries, grapes and berries into a bowl and coat with the lemon juice. Cover and refrigerate.
5. Preheat the oven to 180°C.
6. To make the macaroons, combine the sugar, coconut and egg whites in a bowl and mix.
7. Take teaspoon-size amounts of the mixture and roll into small balls.
8. Place the balls on a baking tray lined with baking paper and press down gently. Do not flatten.
9. Bake the macaroons for 15 minutes, or until they are beginning to brown on top.
10. Allow to cool, then add to the fruit just before serving. Cover with the passionfruit and serve with a dollop of vanilla yoghurt.

Serves 4

Take a heart full of warmth.
Add hugs and kisses.
Sift in your hopes, your
dreams and your wishes.
Blend them together with
laughter and tears.
Add a dash of forgiveness
and stir through the years.
This is the recipe of love.
-Author unknown

Citrus Meringue Pie

pastry
1⅓ cups plain flour
¼ cup icing sugar
130 g butter
3 tbsp water

citrus filling
⅓ cup cornflour
⅓ cup water
½ cup caster sugar
¼ cup desiccated coconut
¼ cup lime juice
¼ cup lemon juice
1 tsp lime zest
1 tsp lemon zest
30 g butter
4 egg yolks

meringue
4 egg whites
¾ cup caster sugar

Like a pavlova, or a sticky date pudding, a meringue pie is a recipe all mums should have. Well, up until now, I didn't. So when we started compiling our lists for this book, I made it my mission to research the meringue pie. In the process, my family has endured so many meringue pies and I have scaled fences and borrowed lemons from local gardens (at odd hours) in order to deliver, what I believe, to be a truly okay citrus meringue pie. You can use a pre-made pastry, but this version is easy and tends to hold the pie together well.
— *Lisa*

1. Preheat the oven to 180°C.
2. To make the pastry, sift together the flour and icing sugar.
3. Using your fingertips, rub the butter into the dry ingredients.
4. When thoroughly combined, add water and use your fingers to work the mixture into a dough.
5. Roll out the dough between two sheets of baking paper to cover a 23 cm springform cake tin.
6. Lay the rolled out pastry dough into the cake tin, trim the edges and refrigerate.
7. After 15 minutes in the fridge, line the pastry with baking paper, then bake blind for 10 minutes in the preheated oven (see Baking Blind, opposite). After 10 minutes, remove the weights and cook for a further 10 minutes. Allow to cool.
8. To make the pie filling, combine the cornflour with a little of the water until smooth.
9. In a saucepan, over a medium heat, combine the remaining water, caster sugar, coconut, juices and zest. When the sugar has dissolved, add the cornflour and stir through over the heat. Continue to stir for a few minutes until the mixture thickens.

10. Remove the pan from the heat and stir through the butter as the mixture starts to cool.
11. Whisk in the egg yolks and refrigerate until completely cooled.
12. To make the meringue, first preheat the oven to 160°C.
13. Place the egg whites in an electric mixer and beat on high until peaks start forming. Add the caster sugar gradually until it has all dissolved and the mix has a thick, glossy appearance.
14. To assemble the pie, pour the cooled citrus filling into the pastry case and top with the meringue. (You can use the back of a spoon to create peaks with the meringue if you like that look.)
15. Bake in the oven for 20 minutes. If not browned, leave for a further 5–10 minutes.
16. Allow to cool to room temperature, then refrigerate.

Serves 8–10

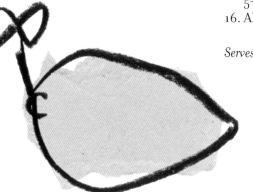

BAKING BLIND
Blind baking is the partial cooking of a pastry prior
to adding the uncooked filling. It prevents sogginess.
Also, in this recipe the citrus filling and meringue
only need a short cooking time, so blind baking ensures
the pastry is cooked through. I keep a container of
rice, which I use for blind baking. I line the pastry
with baking paper, then add the rice. You can also use
dried chickpeas or baking weights.
- Lisa

Lemon Bake

200 g butter, softened
1 cup caster sugar
3 eggs
½ cup milk
1½ cups self-raising flour
1½ tsp baking powder
zest and juice of 2 lemons
⅓ cup granulated sugar

Here's proof that the simple things in life are often the best ...
— *Di*

1. Preheat the oven to 170°C.
2. Beat the butter and sugar in a mixer on high speed until pale and fluffy.
3. Add the eggs, one at a time, followed by the milk, beating until creamy.
4. Sift the flour and baking powder and gradually add to the butter mixture. Finally, add the lemon zest.
5. Transfer the mixture to a lined baking tin (approximately 20 cm × 30 cm × 4 cm) and bake for about 30 minutes, testing the cake with a skewer to ensure that it comes out clean.
6. Remove the cake from the oven and prick with a skewer, covering it with little holes at roughly 2 cm intervals.
7. Combine the lemon juice (approximately ⅓ cup) and granulated sugar in a bowl, then spoon it over the pierced cake.
8. Allow the cake to cool, cut into slices or wedges and serve plain, or with whipped cream for added indulgence.

Serves 12–16

Lib's Fruity Flan

1½ cups self-raising flour, sifted
¾ cup caster sugar
1 egg
1 tsp vanilla essence
125 g butter, melted
1 × 825 g can apricots, drained
1 tsp cinnamon

A one bowl, one spoon wonder, this dessert can be put together in a flash and filled with whatever fruity flavour you fancy. Try plum, apple, mixed frozen berries or your own special combination.
— *Di*

1. Preheat the oven to 180°C.
2. Mix together the flour, sugar, egg, vanilla essence and melted butter in a bowl to form a crumbly dough.
3. Press three-quarters of the mixture into a springform tin. Press some of this mixture up the sides of the tin to encase the filling.
4. Spread your chosen fruit over the cake base and scatter the remaining crumbly mixture over the top. Sprinkle with the cinnamon.
5. Bake in the oven for around 50 minutes, or until the crumble on top is golden. Cool in the tin for 10 minutes before removing.
6. This is especially good served warm with whipped cream and vanilla ice-cream.

Serves 10–12

DE

me dance.

m e ros

OFF THIS PLANET

Di

Acknowledgements

Many thanks to the following wonderful people for all their help, recipes, guidance, modelling, love and support ...

Dorothy, Elise, Yais, Bruce, Trish, Libby, Andy, Renee, Meagan, Sam, The Smyth Family, Corey, Jennifer, RGM, Julie W, Trish, Rupert, Claire, Jude, Chris, Jonathon, Julie, Karen, Kate, Eleisha, Tracy, Fiona, Greg, Astrid, Ryan and his team, and Stephanie.

Recipes are often inspired by other recipes and as such become an interpretation or variation of the original. In particular, we would like to acknowledge the following for providing inspiration in this book:

Hawaiian- and Supreme-style Pizza Scrolls was adapted from of *The Australian Women's Weekly Kids Cooking*, published by ACP Books; Speedy Thai Beef Salad was adapted from Stephanie Alexander's *The Cook's Companion*, published by Viking; Chewy Brown Sugar Pavs was adapted from *Gourmet Traveller*, January 2002; Chocolate Spiders was adapted from a recipe by Chang's Original Fried Noodles.

Index

notes

notes

notes

notes

notes

notes

notes

notes

notes

notes

honey joys

4 cups cornflakes
100 g butter
⅓ cup caster sugar
2 tbsp honey

1. Preheat oven to 160 C and line
   cup cake tins with paper patty pans.
2. Put cornflakes in a large bowl.
3. Melt butter, caster sugar and honey in
   a saucepan over medium heat until frothy.
4. Pour butter mixture over the cornflakes
   and gently mix to thoroughly coat.
5. Spoon cornflake mixture into patty pans
   and bake for 10 minutes. Allow honey
   joys to cool before removing from trays.

Makes approximately 20